S0-BFA-351

Doug Stephens

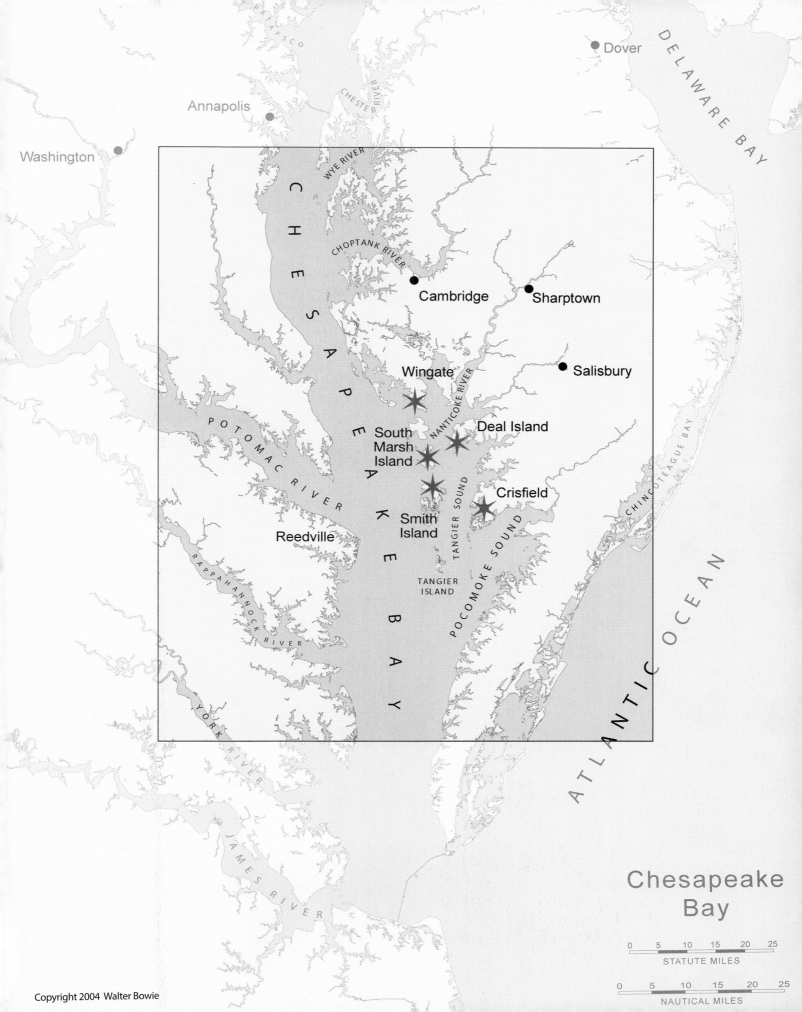

Chesapeake
Bay

Copyright 2004  Walter Bowie

*Jimmy crabs*

*Peelers in a float*

# Summer Harvest

## Portrait of Commercial Crabbing on Chesapeake Bay

*by Doug Stephens*

*Photography by Doug Stephens*

Copyright © 2013 Douglas R. Stephens. All rights
reserved. No part of this publication may be
reproduced, distributed, or transmitted in any
form or by any means, including photocopying,
recording, digital, online, or other electronic or
mechanical methods, without the prior written
permission of the publisher, except in the case
of brief quotations embodied in critical reviews
and  articles and certain other noncommercial
uses permitted by copyright law. For permission
requests, write to:

Doug Stephens
D. Rourke Press
P.O. Box 207
Sharptown, MD 21861
or
SummerHarvest@outlook.com

144 p.     1.9 cm.
ISBN: 978-0-615-87097-7
1. Commercial crabbing–Chesapeake Bay (MD).
2. Blue Crabs.
3. Chesapeake Bay (MD)     I. Title.
Printed in the United States of America.
First edition

Edited by – Victoria Stephens
Layout and Design - Christopher Nelson, Nelson Design

DISTRIBUTED BY D. ROURKE PRESS
For information on promotions, bulk purchases, or
educational use, or to order prints of any of these photos,
please contact SummerHarvest@outlook.com or
P.O. Box 207, Sharptown, MD 21861.

# Dedication

*This book is dedicated to my father, Vic,*

*for making such an outstanding decision*

*to move to the Eastern Shore of Maryland*

*years ago when he was a young man.*

*I'm thankful to him for introducing me to the*

*wonderful world of boating, fishing, crabbing*

*and exploring the Chesapeake Bay and its*

*tributaries. These are memories I will always*

*cherish. I would also like to thank him for being*

*such a good role model for me by teaching*

*me honesty, integrity and hard work.*

———————— ◆ ◆ ◆ ————————

# Acknowledgments

This is a look into the working lives of commercial watermen who make their living crabbing on Chesapeake Bay and its tributaries.

My deepest thanks to:

   Captain Harry Windsor

   Captain Robert "Nussie" Webster

   Captain Lowell J. "Tall Man" Moore

   Captain Stevie Webster

Thanks to Carrie Connelly for having mercy on a poor, starving artist in her frame shop a long, long time ago.

Thanks to Whitey Schmidt for early encouragement and showing me the path to make this book happen.

Thanks to Jim and Marge Miller at Vista Photo Inc. in Odenton, MD for their professional color transparency scanning service.

Thanks to Chris Nelson for his artist's eye and superb layout and design skills.

And thanks to my sister, Victoria, for her editing and art direction skills, insights and keen eye.

Special thanks to Captain Nussie Webster for allowing me into his busy life, patiently answering my many questions, and for being a willing participant in this project.

Other books by Doug Stephens:
*Workin' With the Wind: Portrait of a Chesapeake Bay Skipjack* (2004)

# Summer Harvest

## Portrait of Commercial Crabbing on Chesapeake Bay

The roadside produce stand is a staple of the Eastern Shore.

Local sweet corn;
a "must have"
for crab feasts.

# Introduction

Some of my earliest childhood recollections go back to spending time on Chesapeake Bay with my father and my brothers, Chris and Bill. Dad would take us fishing in his old wooden fishing boat. I distinctly remember the boat ramp at Deal Island. A quaint little fishing village, Deal Island is located about three quarters of the way down the Eastern Shore of Maryland and overlooks a spectacular body of water known as Tangier Sound. The long, scenic ride through the marsh, the smell of salt water, the seagulls soaring overhead and the wooden work boats moored in the marina are memories permanently etched in my mind.

Usually, while Dad and one of his buddies launched the boat or while they were loading it up, Chris and I would look for crabs to net along the bulkheads and pilings. Dad also took us to places in Tangier Sound where the water was six to ten feet deep. We would tie pieces of raw chicken necks to hand lines, lower them into the water, and then fasten the lines around the boat. Chris and I would periodically check each line, pulling it in to see if there was a crab hanging onto the end. If there was, an urgent call went out. "I got one, get the net!" This method of catching crabs is what we call "chicken neckin.'"

Guided by Dad and his good friend, Uly Mentasti, we often ventured throughout the shallow waters off Smith and South Marsh Islands. We'd wade through the waste deep water, looking for soft crabs to catch. The water was crystal clear back then, and we could actually see the crabs on the bottom. On other occasions, while fishing in deep water along a channel, an occasional crab would swim by the boat along the surface of the water. Somebody would usually grab the net to scoop it up so we could check it out.

Then there is eating crabs! Crab feasts have long been a summer time tradition of family and friends on the Delmarva Peninsula and the entire Chesapeake Bay area. There is nothing better than digging in and getting your hands messy while enjoying the delicious, sweet meat of the Chesapeake Bay blue crab. The crab is often complimented with a variety of fresh, locally grown produce – white sweet corn, cantaloupe, watermelon, vine ripened tomatoes and more.

Generations continue to enjoy this tradition. My daughter Amanda and my young nieces and nephews have become quite adept at "cleaning" the crabs, their small fingers easily getting at the tasty tidbits of meat. We each have our own way of cleaning and eating steamed crabs, but it is Amanda who tickles me when she cleans crab. She picks out and soaks the meat in vinegar for a few minutes, accumulating a nice portion of the succulent white meat. She then dips a bite of crab in seafood seasoning before eating it. This method never would have worked while I was growing up. With five kids in the family, someone would have pilfered the prized meat before it was eaten by the person who was piling it up! A crab feast is more that just eating crabs. It is a social event and in my extended family, an important one. Even though we are now spread out all over the country, whenever we get together on the Eastern Shore in the summer season, we have a crab feast. It's tradition!

Everyone in my family loves to cook, and there was no one better at it than my mother, Laurie. Even though she wasn't originally from the Eastern Shore, she made the best fried soft crabs I have ever eaten. Seasoned perfectly, cooked crispy on the outside and tender on the inside, they were delicious. Fortunately for me, her recipe was handed down, and my wife Nancy has mastered it. Many times we have invited company over for a dinner of soft crabs. More than once, our guests let us know that they don't eat soft crabs. "Have you ever had Nancy's fried soft crabs?" I ask. "No," is their usual reply. Well, after the soft crabs are sampled out of courtesy, a second helping is rarely turned down. In fact, we are yet to have leftover soft crabs.

Because I have been catching and eating crabs all my life, I thought I knew a lot about them. But after meeting Captain Robert "Nussie" Webster and his grandfather, Captain Harry Windsor, I came to realize how little I did know. While combining my interest in photography and the Chesapeake Bay and its tributaries, my eyes have been opened to some of the fascinating, colorful, and intricate characteristics of the Chesapeake Bay blue crab, the different methods used to harvest them, and the people who catch them.

This is their story.

# One

## Windsor's Marina

One afternoon in late July 1984, I sat in my pickup truck at Wenona Harbor on Deal Island, waiting for Captain Dicky Webster to return from a fishing party aboard the *Standor III*, a thirty-six foot bay boat. Captain Dicky's sailing vessel, the working Skipjack, the *Caleb W. Jones* (an oyster dredger), was foremost on my mind.

A little time passed before Captain Ted Webster, Dicky's brother, powered in with his fishing party, loaded with a cooler full of large trout. As I continued to wait for Captain Dicky, a guy named Bernie rode up on his moped. I had met Bernie two weeks earlier on a fishing trip with Captain Dicky, Jim Coffman, Steve Eccleston, Don Fountain, Rodney Pierson, and John Gordy aboard the *Standor III*. Bernie was first mate at the time.

Anyway, Bernie pulled up to my truck, came to a stop, and we began to talk. I told him about my photography work with Captain Dicky and the *Caleb* and expressed my interest in photographing some crabbers. Being the good natured soul he is, Bernie said, "Go introduce yourself to Nussie (pronounced Nus-e) across the Deal Island Bridge and to the right. That's coming from Wenona. Tell em' you're a friend of Don Fountain."

A few days later, I took Bernie's advice and set off. As I neared the marina, I couldn't help but notice two signs along the road. One read: Peelers – Crabs – Live – Frozen – Soft crabs – Hard Crabs - Open. The other: Crabs. Windsor's Marina. "Crabs, crabs, crabs. This must be the place," I said to myself.

The property was neat as a pin and extremely photogenic. It had WELCOME written all over it. A relatively small harbor, the basin was nicely enclosed by a bulkhead and had an opening on the southeast side. A few young weeping willows, spaced inter-mittently along the shoreline, were well on their way to becoming wonderful shade trees. About twenty-five boats filled the slips.

Along the bulkhead on the north side were two covered crab shanties. I could just see the floats inside – raised wooden tables with sides, filled with salt water and crabs. A big, old white house with an attached garage stood guard. But it was the little white bait shack that overlooked the harbor that caught my eye and my interest. Two windows hinged from the top were held open with old weathered ropes. Above one window there was another sign: Peelers – Soft Crabs – Hard Crabs.

*The property was neat as a pin and had WELCOME written all over it.*

As I got out of the truck, a guy about my age stepped out of one of the crab shanties. He wore blue jeans, a tee shirt and a Dukes Lumber baseball cap. I suspected the cap was probably a gift from my friend Don Fountain, who works for Dukes. The man had a dark tan, obviously from many hours in the sun. Beside him was a little brown and white dog. The dog was just a waggin' his tail, as happy as can be.

"Are you Nussie?" I asked.

His one word response: "Yep."

For a fleeting moment, a feeling of unease washed over me. I thought, "This guy doesn't know me from a hole in the wall." Then I remembered Bernie's advice. "I'm a friend of Don Fountain's." I went on to tell him about my work with Captain Dicky. "Do you think I could go out on the water with you to take some pictures while you work?" I asked. Sure enough, Bernie was right. Since I knew Don Fountain, I was no stranger.

Nussie answered right away, "No problem. We sail aboard the boat over there and leave before daybreak on most days." Nussie pointed to a boat moored along the bulkhead. The name along its bow read, *Miss Julie*. I thanked him and we talked for a while. I discovered that Nussie was just a year older than me and we had both studied masonry under the same instructor during high school. We had lots to talk about.

Captain Robert
"Nussie" Webster

*Windsor's Marina*

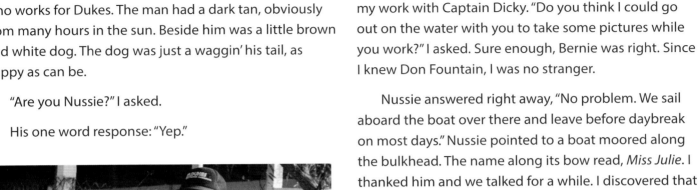

Before I left, we walked over to the window of the little white bait shack. The interior was sparse. There were two heavily used upholstered chairs and what looked like a couple of fifty-year-old refrigerators. A little side table next to the chairs held a can of mosquito repellent. A few fishing rigs hung from a nail on the wall. The sales counter separated the seating area from the exterior. Seated in one of the chairs was the little brown and white dog. In the chair next to him was an elderly gentleman. Nussie introduced me to his grandfather as a friend of Don Fountain's, and explained I was interested in taking pictures.

Nussie's grandfather got up out of his chair and reached out his hand. "I'm Cap'n Harry," he said with a smile, and firmly shook my hand.

With introductions complete, I sketched out my time spent photographing Captain Dicky and the *Caleb W. Jones*, and expressed my interest in photographing some crabbers.

"You've come to the right place for that!" said Captain Harry.

"Great!" I replied and smiled, my unease now completely subsided.

"What's the name of your four-legged friend?" I asked.

"Suzie," answered Captain Harry. His tone relayed how much he cared for the dog. Our conversation was short and I thanked them both before I left.

On my way home, I thought, "Now, those are some really nice guys -- and what a wonderful place!" From that first day, Captain Harry Windsor and Captain Robert "Nussie" Webster welcomed me into their fascinating world of crabs, no questions asked.

I quickly learned that these men possess extraordinary expertise and knowledge of working the waters of Chesapeake Bay in search of crabs, fish and oysters, and that their skills have been passed from generation to generation. I also came to understand why they are so well respected and liked in their community. They are hard working gentlemen. An additional bonus for me was that this would be the beginning of a lifelong friendship.

*The Miss Julie*

# Two

## Captain Nussie Webster

The first time I rode with Captain Nussie Webster to photograph a Chesapeake Bay crabber at work, I was surprised that I already knew his first mate. Hal Thomas and I were classmates in the masonry program at the Vocational-Technical School in Salisbury, Maryland for two years. We had butted heads a few times at school, so it was an awkward moment when we saw each other at Windsor's Marina. But we shook hands and said hello with no mention of our past difficulties. In fact, Hal was very pleasant throughout the day and we got along fine.

The weather was a different story. The drive from Salisbury was miserable. The fog was "thick as butter," making the journey to Windor's 30 minutes longer than usual. Good thing I gave myself extra travel time. The first light of day was breaking as I pulled into the parking lot, but even so, when I got out of the truck, I couldn't see past the bulkhead basin of the marina. The air was humid. No wind at all – not so much as a breath of air stirring.

Nussie and Hal readied the boat with the day's supplies and equipment while I ambled around the harbor and boats taking a few pictures. What a still morning. It felt surreal. The only things visible were the docks, boats and the surrounding bulkhead. Past the little marine basin was a wall of dense fog.

When Nussie motioned he was ready to shove off, I boarded the *Miss Julie*. The fog had begun to lift. Captain Nussie had been waiting for the moment when he could see well enough to proceed safely.

Visibility improved quickly as we made our way out of the basin. We sailed under the Deal Island Bridge. To the left was Deal Island Harbor, a small harbor with ten or fifteen boat slips and boats of all sizes and shapes, a Skipjack and marine police boat among them.

The county boat ramp my father used when I was a kid was next, then the place that Dad and I used to buy fishing bait. Captain Nussie mentioned the business had changed its name to Island Seafood.

Effortlessly we sailed past the breakwater.

While leaving the slip and going through Deal Island Harbor, Nussie steered the boat from a place closer to the stern, on the starboard side. Once out on open water, while the boat was still in gear and moving, he walked to the cabin and took control of the boat from the steering wheel inside, where he stayed until we reached our destination – the crabbing grounds.

*A dreamlike feeling engulfed me as I looked out the opening of the marina basin, only to see a wall of fog.*

*Morning fog & boats*

It was still barely light when Nussie and Hal put on oil skins (waterproof coveralls) and left the cabin. Nussie stepped out of the cabin and went back to the controls at the stern while Hal prepped the gear. Once back at the tiller, Nussie steared for his first crab pot. Hal was positioned farther forward between the cabin and the engine box.

The sun was just beginning its daily trek across the sky as we approached the first float, which indicated where the first crab pot was, under the water. Nussie grabbed a long boat hook and reached for the line connecting the float to the crab pot. He then pulled the line hard enough to get some slack and wrapped it around a stainless steel wheel powered by hydraulics. He explained that the winder was one of the best improvements in the crabbing business. "We used to pull these pots by hand," Nussie said. "That was some kind of hard work." Seeing how difficult it was just to get enough slack in the line to put the rope on the winder, I wholeheartedly agreed.

*I could see the men's discomfort while shaking the pot as some of the jellyfish's stinging tentacles reached their arms and faces.*

Nussie pulled the lever that controlled the winder and in came the crab pot. Because it was still relatively dark, I needed the flash on my camera and quickly attached it as the first pot came in.

Much to my surprise, grass grew all over the pot. Nussie said this was normal, that the grass grows all summer and the pots get heavier as the summer progresses.

When the crab pot reached the surface, Nussie grabbed it and in one fluid motion, swung it up on a small platform that was resting on the boat's washboard.

In addition to the grass, the pot was loaded with jellyfish. As the pot landed with a thud on the board, several jellyfish oozed out between the mesh wires of the pot and landed in a gooey mess.

*It was Hal's job to "cull" or sort the crabs while Captain Nussie maneuvered the Miss Julie to the next crab pot.*

This is where Hal stepped in. Nussie opened the crab pot and the two men lifted and shook the pot to empty its contents into a wooden box located behind the platform that was resting on the washboard. This was the culling box, a little smaller than a crab pot. A few crabs dropped out along with the remaining jellyfish. I could see the men's discomfort as they shook the pot. Jellyfish's stinging tentacles reached their arms and faces, making the heavy work even more difficult. "It's part of the job," Nussie said with a sigh.

It was then Hal's job to "cull" or sort the crabs while Captain Nussie maneuvered his 32-foot bay boat, the *Miss Julie*, to the next crab pot. Hal had a measuring device in hand and a couple of bushel baskets situated on the engine box. He said, "Hard crabs go into one basket, the peelers into another." (Peelers are hard crabs showing signs of getting ready to shed into a soft crab.) Every once in a while, he grabbed a crab and walked what he called a "buster" over to the other side of the boat and placed it in a large wooden box divided into sections and partially filled with water. (A buster is a peeler that is in the final phase of shedding its hard shell.) Finally, the undersized crabs were returned to the Bay. This was fascinating. Other than size, how could he tell

which crab was which, I wondered. As I later found out, it takes several years, many questions and plenty of observation.

The men moved quickly. Nussie skippered the *Miss Julie* to the next pot. Same process – hook the line, wrap it onto the winder, pull in the pot, dump its contents. Hal culled while Nussie maneuvered the boat to the next crab pot. They didn't miss a beat. Nussie's skill at the helm was a pleasure to watch. His concentration on the task at hand – unrelenting. It was a well coordinated operation.

The morning continued the same way, pot after pot, jellyfish after jellyfish, a few crabs in between. There were some crabs caught this day, but not many. Nussie explained it was normal for this time of year. "The 'doubler' run is long over, the grass builds up, the crab pots get heavier, and there's more jellyfish to annoy us. Harder work, less crabs. That's the way it is in late summer. It's not prime time for peelers." Nussie continued, "And its peelers we're after." At the end of the long day, we headed back to Windsor's where Nussie and Hal placed the peelers and busters in floats, 4'x8' raised containers with circulated bay water. The hard crabs were refrigerated in the cooler to be sold later.

*Nussie's skill at the helm was obvious. His concentration at the task at hand – unrelenting.*

As the men finished up, I thought about the day's catch, all the hard work and all the stinging jellyfish splashing on the men's arms and faces. "Not as easy as one would imagine," I said to myself.

When the day started, I didn't realize we were going after peelers. All I knew was that I was going crabbing. What little I knew about peelers was that they shed into tasty soft crabs and that they were good for bait. I had much to learn.

The day had been relatively slow and the hazy weather wasn't ideal for photography, but we caught some crabs, and I found the day to be interesting and enjoyable. Captain Nussie's soft spoken, easy going way and Hal's cooperation made the voyage that much better.

With the unloading of the catch complete, it was time to go. I had been up since 4:00 a.m. and was getting tired. Unlike the crabbers, I was not used to getting up so early. I said my farewells and invited myself back for another trip. "No problem," was Nussie's reply. "Anytime."

"Nothing ever seems to be a problem for Nussie," I thought to myself.

*The busters and peelers close to shedding were placed in a large wooden box that was divided into sections and partially filled with water.*

# Three

## Late in the Season

Within a week I was back. This time, the weather was perfect. I had called Nussie the night before and confirmed the open invitation. The weatherman was predicting clear skies, light winds and lower humidity. "We leave the harbor about 5:30 a.m.," Nussie said.

*"The buildup of the grass on the pots is a good thing. The crabs look for a place to hide when they're gettin' ready to shed."*

When I arrived, Nussie and Hal were ready to go. The day's first light was in the making and there were crabs to be caught. What a beautiful morning! The weatherman's forecast was on the money. Same as last time, away we went with Captain Nussie at the helm. There is a special feeling one gets when sailing out of a marina at the first light of day. It doesn't matter if you are on a work boat, sail boat, private fishing boat, or dinghy. It is an event to be experienced. It is an occasion that will give the participant everlasting fond memories. Vivid colors are magnified. Peacefulness is unending. The anticipation of a new day with all its possibilities is exhilarating. Combined, these things make getting up in the middle of the night well worthwhile.

*We reached the crabbing grounds and the men went to work.*

On this particular day, it didn't matter to me if we caught crabs. The ride out had already made my trip worthwhile. "These guys do this day after day," I thought to myself, "hoping to go out, catch some crabs and make some money. What a commute." We reached the crabbing grounds and the men went to work.

The first thing I noticed was that the jellyfish weren't as abundant as my last outing. Nussie nonchalantly said, "Some days are worse than others." I could see that the grass was continuing to grow on the crab pots. Nussie explained, "The buildup of grass on the pots is a good thing. The crabs look for a place to hide when they're gettin' ready to shed. That's why, even though they're heavier, we don't usually pull the pots and power wash 'em clean 'til the end of the season."

It's a funny thing out there. One crab pot comes up empty and the very next one can have fifteen to twenty crabs in it. Again, each time a pot was emptied into the culling box, first mate Hal would carefully go through its contents, crab by crab. He kept looking at the crabs' backfins for signs and sorted the crabs accordingly. Hal showed me a few examples of each sign, but I could not see what he was trying to show me.

Hal put most of the crabs into the hard crab basket. A few went into the peeler basket and an occasional buster was placed in the tank with water in it. I quickly recognized the busters, since they are distinctive as they begin the process of coming out of or "shedding" their old shells. I could see the edges of the soft shell crab underneath the hard shell on top. The remaining undersized crabs were returned to Tangier Sound.

The morning wore on and the trend became obvious. I asked Nussie, "I thought we were trying to catch peelers. Why are we catching more hard crabs than peelers?"

"It's like this every year," he replied. "Peeler season is best in late spring and early summer. Especially during the doubler run. It drops off after that."

I told him that on occasion, while fishing with my father, I had seen doubler crabs swimming near the surface of the water but that was the extent of what I knew about them. I can only guess Nussie was getting more accustomed to my questions and my camera in his face because he began to tell me about the doubler run.

*These guys do this day after day hoping to go out, catch some crabs, and make some money.*

*Hal kept looking at the crabs' backfins for signs and sorted the crabs accordingly.*

*Peelers*

*Nussie hooked the crab pots, floats and line with a considerable amount of effort.*

"We used to pull these pots by hand."

"It usually starts in mid to late May, when the moon is comin' on full and the water is gettin' warm. And it seems like it's all at once." He went on to say, "During the doubler run, when the she crab or Sook [Nussie calls the females "she" crabs] gets ready to shed, she looks for a Jimmy [male crab] to mate with. It is only while she's soft that she can mate with the Jimmy. The she crab is vulnerable during this phase. So, in addition to mating, the Jimmy protects her from gettin' eaten by other crabs or fish 'til she once again becomes a hard crab."

"That's a pretty good reason to look for a mate," I replied.

"You'll have to come down in the spring to see for yourself," he said.

*"You want a piece of me?"*

Back at Windsor's Marina, Nussie and Hal unloaded the day's catch from the *Miss Julie* while I checked out the floats Nussie used to shed the crabs. The process of catching hard crabs and putting them in water in floats until they shed their shells and become soft crabs is referred to as "shedding crabs." The floats were built about waist high and in four-foot by eight-foot sections. Two sections of floats were covered with a pole-type structure and another two were out in the open. Water was pumped in from the marina basin and distributed throughout the floats through two or three spray nozzles per float. The water flowed out through two drains in the middle of each section. There was growth on the sides and bottom, making the water a little murky, so it was difficult to see the crabs in the water.

Nussie explained the floats get cloudy late in the season because of algae growth on the sides and bottom of the floats and that if the water is churned up at the intake in the marina basin, it will be cloudy in the floats. He went on to say it's usually clear otherwise.

As the men finished their tasks, I was again told to come back for another visit in the spring. "Check on us in early May," Nussie said.

"You can count on that," was my response. "I look forward to it."

After the winder pulls the pot to the surface, Nussie brings it in the rest of the way by hand.

# Four

## Lowell J. Moore, a/k/a Tall Man

was exhibiting and selling my photographs in art shows throughout the Eastern Shore area and as far west as Sandy Point State Park on the northwestern side of the Chesapeake. My intention was to sell photographs, period. I had what I thought was a nice inventory of Skipjack and oyster dredging photos, a few crabbing pictures and a portable wall to display them. Up to that point, most of my work had focused on the working Skipjack, the *Caleb W. Jones* and its Captain, Dicky Webster.

It was late winter and there I was at an art show and sale in the old Salisbury Mall. Out of the blue, a guy came up to me, took a look at my work and said, "I know Dicky Webster." He continued as he looked over my photographs, "Dicky's a good man."

The guy was over six feet tall and lanky, with a weathered face and broad smile. Friendly as a man could be. We talked for a long time about life on the water, catching crabs and oysters, and fishing on the Bay. He had obviously spent his life on the water. He told me about a few working Skipjacks that sailed out of the area he is from in Dorchester County. I mentioned Nussie and his peeler potting business and that I had started to go with him to take pictures. Without hesitation he said, "I'm a crabber from down in Wingit, and you're more than welcome to come trotlining with me." The idea of building on the enjoyable and productive adventures I had with Nussie appealed to me. Another crabber to photograph, and a trotliner, too!

Where's Wingit?" I asked.

"It's south of Cambridge, between Toddville and Crocheron," he answered.

"And your name?"

"Lowell J. Moore, but most people call me Tall Man." He flashed his big smile again. "Come on down for a visit some time."

Lowell J. Moore, a/k/a Tall Man

Tall Man and the Bonnie Rose

The waterman sorting crabs
in the little white shanty.

Nussie shows me a "buster."

# *Five*

## Fishin' Up

It was May when I next visited Windsor's Marina, where I found Nussie and Captain Harry hard at work in the little white shanty. They were sorting soft crabs according to size. They put some of the crabs into wooden box trays and some into heavy plastic trays. After sorting, the trays were placed in the old refrigerator. That job completed, the men headed out to the crab floats by the edge of the harbor. It was time to search the individual floats for the peeler crabs that had just shed into soft crabs. This they called "fishin' up."

Nussie turned the water running into the floats down to a trickle, one float at a time, to see the crabs easier. He was right. The water was crystal clear in the spring with no build up of growth and mud. The sun was shining and reflecting on the water and the floats were all painted up and looking good. But it was the crabs that caught my attention. They were vivid blue and green and most had red tips on their claws. What a beautiful display of Mother Nature's colorful creations.

Before they started fishin' up at each float, the men counted the sheds to keep record of how many soft crabs were in the float since the last time the float was fished up. Then they got started. Captain Harry held an unusual looking net he used to scoop up the soft crabs. The net was about nine inches in diameter with tight webbing and no basket to speak of. This was attached to a pole about a foot and a half long. Captain Harry

explained he could reach the crabs better with the net and his hands wouldn't be in water all morning. When he did pull out a soft crab, he also pulled out what he called a shed, the leftover exoskeleton after the crab molted or shed its shell to become a soft crab. The shed was of no use or value and was put in a separate basket to be discarded later.

Nussie pulled a crab out of the water that was in the middle of the shedding process - a "buster" crab.

*"Count the number of sheds and that's how many soft crabs you'll have."*

*Green peeler crabs get put in floats in the back.*

It was amazing how much larger the soft crabs were than the shells they emerged from. The men patiently explained, "It's not unusual for the larger crabs to get hung up at this point." Sure enough, some died in the process. "The bigger the crab, the more likely it is to get hung up in the shed," Nussie told me.

This all seemed simple enough. But there was more going on here than just removing the soft crabs that had recently shed out. Nussie was closely inspecting some of the peelers that, as yet, were still hard crabs.

"What are you looking for?" I asked.

"Signs," was Nussie's reply.

"Ah, Hal tried to show me these signs on our last trip." The signs were difficult to recognize, and I had not yet picked up the skill.

As he held a crab, Nussie thoughtfully said, "Look, right here on the backfin, there is a little red line. Can you see it?" I looked closely, couldn't see a thing and told him so. "This line here first appears as white and as the crab gets closer to sheddin', it turns red."

The crab looked to me like any other crab. I knew Nussie could tell I wasn't able to detect any line, white or red. With patience and sincerity, he said, "It takes time to learn how to read a crab." No brag. Just a simple fact.

Nussie placed a bushel basket directly in the water. "Why are you putting some of the crabs in the basket?" I asked.

"The crabs that are closest to shedding are put in a separate float up front. We get to them first the next time we fish up because if you get to a soft crab too late, it will start to get hard again. They're buckrams and they're not much good to most people. The green peelers or crabs farthest from sheddin' get put in the floats in the back." His astute knowledge of his business was astounding.

*Looking for signs*

There were lots of crab pots lined up around the marina next to the floats that weren't under cover. Nussie told me that he would be setting those pots out "soon as doubler season is kickin' in." I noticed more floats tied to the dock. These floats also held crabs – Jimmy crabs that Nussie "baits" his pots with. He reminded me about the females that look for the Jimmy crabs before shedding. Amazing.

Nussie went on to say that for years, everybody used to shed crabs in floats like these. That's where they got the name "floats." Then, one day, somebody came up with the idea of moving them onto land and pumping water through them, greatly increasing accessibility. Good idea. Extremely hard and time consuming work, made slightly easier. Still darn hard work, though.

*With the water turned down to a trickle, I could easily see the beautiful crabs in the crystal clear water.*

*Bait for the peeler pots*

## Six

## Bank Traps

**W**hen Nussie told me that the doubler season would probably be coming in soon, I knew my return to Windsor's was just around the corner. Within days, I was back to find Nussie and another waterman named Johnny Mister working on the crab pots that were stacked next to the floats. Hal was nowhere to be seen and just like that, Johnny was now Nussie's first mate.

Like everything else in life, there is a lot more to commercial crabbing than meets the eye. Come to find out, in order for the watermen to keep their expensive crab pots in usable condition for as long as possible, the owner has to perform regular maintenance on them.

At the end of each season and as seen on my previous outings in August, when the crab pots are removed from the floor of Tangier Sound, they come out of the water covered with a growth of sea grass. Nussie said the growth isn't a bad thing at the end of the season, because the crabs are looking for a place to hide before shedding. But, this is not the case in the spring season when the crab pots are baited with live Jimmy crabs. The females need to be able to see the Jimmy crabs. In addition, the crab pots get quite heavy with excess growth and require considerably more energy to move them. And so, at the end of each season, or at a minimum before the start of a new season, Nussie power washes the crab pots to get rid of the excess growth.

*Working on the crab pots*

*Johnny Mister, the new first mate*

Once that task was completed , Nussie and Johnny inspected each pot, replacing missing or worn out parts, wire brushing certain places or just bending the crab pot back into its correct shape. They attached zinc bars to each corner to help prevent corrosion from salt water, then added little C-clips to the corners for structural reinforcement. After that, they replaced the round plastic lids that cover the bait compartments, if needed. The elastic cords that secure the bait compartment lids and the hatch that opens to remove the crabs were next. The men then attached floats with long cords strong enough to withstand a considerable amount of pressure. Violent storms with strong winds and high waves put this component to the test. All this work was done with a large amount of kneeling, bending, stooping and lifting. Movements that require a lot of energy and are backbreaking! Finally, the pots were lined up with the floats sticking out, waiting for a new coat of paint. Of particular note, each float is painted with a personal color so the waterman can distinguish whose crab pots are whose. In Nussie's case, the color was maroon.

Several hours later, Captain Harry showed up. It was time for Nussie and Johnny to take a break from working on the crab pots. They said we were going to check on the bank traps. "What's a bank trap?" I wondered.

All four of us climbed aboard an old wooden skiff tied to the dock. It was located behind the hard crab floats. We sailed off with Captain Harry at the helm. The boat could have used a coat of paint but definitely did the job. She was sturdy and the little Johnson motor never missed a beat. Like the men aboard, not fancy but hard working.

*En route to the bank traps*

Once out of the marina basin, Captain Harry headed east. After a short distance, he navigated the skiff into a long creek. We rode for five or ten minutes before we reached the bank trap. The Captain slowed the boat to a crawl as we approached what looked like a wire fence about half way across the creek. The fence was shaped like a shallow V and had the equivalent of an oversized crab pot at the crux of the V. The big wire cage was a cube about four feet by four feet. When I looked closer, I realized it was an oversized crab pot!

The men had obviously worked together at this task before. Captain Harry maneuvered the boat to where it needed to be and kept it steady. When we glided up to the pot, Nussie and Johnny disconnected it from the wire fence. Nussie and Johnny wrestled the heavy crab pot in without tipping over the skiff. Their movements were sure and strong, as if they had performed this chore together a million times before.

*Bank trap*

*They pulled the crabs out and slid them into a large metal wash tub and a bushel basket.*

The pot held a good many crabs and although they didn't say so, the men seemed pleased. Unlike dumping a crab pot aboard the *Miss Julie*, they slowly pulled the crabs out and slid them into a large metal wash tub and a bushel basket. The smallest ones were returned to the creek and swam away. It seemed the trip was a smashing success.

*As they read the crabs for signs, they put them into one or the other of three bushel baskets.*

*Although they didn't say so,
the men seamed pleased.*

On the way back to Windsor's, Nussie and Johnny went through the crabs one by one. As they read the crabs for signs, they put them into one or another of three bushel baskets. Nussie said, "One basket is for rank peelers or crabs with red bands. These are the crabs real close to sheddin'. One basket is for white banded peelers and the third is for the green crabs. Green crabs are the crabs that aren't showing any signs of sheddin'." He went on to say, "In the spring, the crabs start sheddin' in the shallows of the creeks a week or two before the crabs in the deeper water of Tangier Sound." It wasn't until years later that I learned this method of catching crabs had been one of the best kept secrets on the island for a long time. People often wondered how Nussie and Captain Harry were able to catch soft crabs before almost anyone else.

Back at the dock, the catch was put into the floats according to where the crabs stood in the shedding process. The ones closest to shedding were put up front, and the green crabs were placed in the back and so on.

That task complete, Nussie and Johnny went back to working on the crab pots. Captain Harry found his favorite chair in the shanty overlooking the harbor.

# Seven

## Goin' Fishin'

*Jim Coffman shows off a real nice trout.*

t wasn't the crack of dawn, but the day was still early when my good friend Jim Coffman and I made our way to Windsor's Marina. We were going fishing. My boat, the *Cash Flow*, was moored at the marina.

The *Cash Flow* is a 20-foot Grady White that was given to me by my father. It needed some work at the time. I had it re-powered with a new engine and Jim helped me put the rest of the boat back into "ship shape."

During my previous visits to Windsor's, I noticed a few empty boat slips and inquired about renting one. As usual, "No problem" was the answer I received.

I have rented a slip there just about every year since then. The cost? Nominal in relation to the benefits. Keeping my boat in the water and not hauling it back and forth by trailer made going fishing much more enjoyable. Just jump in, untie four lines and go.

*Working the edge of the channel*

*Nussie zeroes in on the next crab pot*

*Pulling pots*

We got the fishing report and our bait from Captain Harry and headed out to Tangier Sound. We fished for a few hours and picked up some nice trout. Jim caught a 3- to 4-pound beauty. It was around 9:30 a.m. when I told Jim I'd like to find Nussie and take a few pictures of him at work aboard the *Miss Julie* from a different perspective. After a short but enjoyable fifteen minute boat ride, we found Nussie and the *Miss Julie* working the eastern edge of the channel. Johnny was aboard, and they were hard at it, pulling crab pots.

The morning sky was perfectly clear and the winds were light. Nussie was wearing his dark green oilskins and Johnny had a bright yellow apron to protect him

from getting soaked. Johnny wore a sweat shirt and Nussie a flannel, as the air was still a little cool. We got close enough to say hello while making sure we didn't get in the way.

Jimmy took the wheel of the *Cash Flow* while I snapped off pictures. We circled Nussie and the *Miss Julie* several times to photograph them at work from different angles. The men and their boat worked together like one well tuned machine – each man knew his next task. The crab pots seemed to be everywhere and Jimmy avoided getting us tangled up in the crab lines.

*We didn't stay long, and before we headed back to Windsor's, we wished them good luck.*

As far as the eye could see across the water, there were crab pot floats. I then understood the need for color coding the floats. We observed some crabs in the pots as the men pulled them up and it was good to see that the men were having some success with their intended catch. We didn't stay long. Before we headed back to Windsor's, we wished them good luck.

MISS JULIE
CHANCE MD

# Eight

## Prepping the *Bonnie Rose*

I decided to make my way to Wingit, south of Cambridge. Subsequent to turning off Route 50, it came to mind to check my map to make sure I was on the right path. After what seemed like ten minutes of searching the map for a place called Wingit, I finally realized there is no such place. I recalled Lowell J. Moore's heavy Eastern Shore accent and with a smile, I realized that my destination was Wingate, Maryland.

After a long ride down a winding road with marsh grass and wetlands on either side, I found the little community of Wingate and looked for the marina. Incredibly, the first person I met up with was Lowell J. Moore. There he was, electric sander in hand, refinishing the exterior of his boat. His helper was following behind him, painting the white section of the hull above the water line.

I got out of my pickup to greet them and the first thing Lowell did was introduce me as his good friend from Salisbury. It was as though we had known each other for years. Lowell invited me to spend time with them so we could talk while they finished their project. He explained that in Dorchester County, trotlining is the only method used to catch crabs commercially. The watermen who used crab pots to catch crabs had to stay in Somerset County, which is why, when crossing Tangier Sound, the crab pot floats come to an abrupt end at the county line. I also learned that hard crab season started later than peeler season.

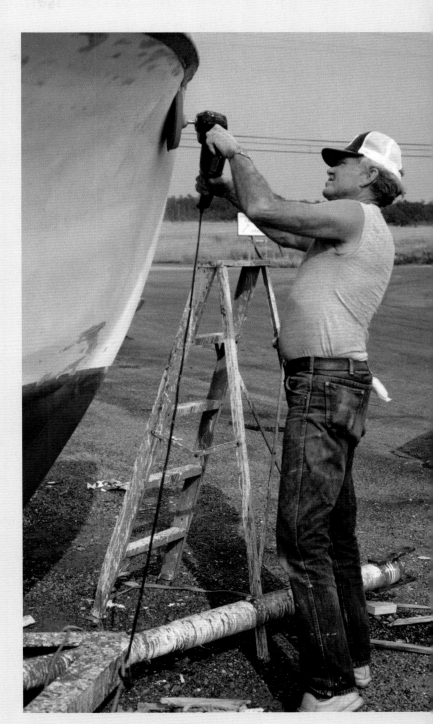

*Tall Man working on the Bonnie Rose*

*Painting the hull
above the waterline*

*A fine boat indeed*

45955

BONNIE ROSE

Other men stopped by to pass the time of day or ask a question or two during my visit. Each man addressed Lowell by the name Tall Man. As before, Tall Man introduced me to everyone as "my good friend from Salisbury." Before I knew it, and from that day forward, I too refer to Lowell J. Moore as "Tall Man." It seems fitting considering his height of well over six feet.

I wandered around to the stern of the boat and saw the name *Bonnie Rose* in big white letters on a brown background. "I named her after my wife," Tall Man proudly told me.

My timing was perfect, as it wasn't long before they had finished up. The boat was ready to go for the season and she looked first-class! The bottom was painted blue and the sides white. The thin red lines in between set her off nicely. The top side trim was brown to match the stern and there was one black stripe all the way around at the rub rail. A fine boat indeed.

Tall Man mentioned, "Most days I leave the harbor at 5:00 a.m. You'll want to be here around a quarter of. Why don't you come back and we'll go crabbin'?"

"I will indeed," I replied.

*"I named her after my wife."*

BONNIE ROSE

WINGATE MD

We said our goodbyes and for the rest of the day, I went on to explore the area. I checked out Wingate and found my way to Bishops Head, Toddville and Crocheron. A photographers dream!

# Nine

## First Doubler Run

N ussie called me on a Wednesday evening. In his typical calm demeanor and slow drawl, he said, "You may want to come on down…now." I was back at Windsor's at 4:45 the next morning.

I wanted to be there early and was delighted I did so. When I arrived, I could feel the excitement in the air. The place was lit up like a Christmas tree. All the lights were on in the bait and shedding shanties. I saw Nussie and Captain Harry fishin' up, and made my way over to them. What a sight! The floats were jam-packed! Crabs everywhere. The floats themselves seemed to be alive. What a sight to see! Nussie and Captain Harry were moving faster than I had ever seen them move. Their urgency was obvious.

"They're sheddin' all at once," Nussie quietly said with a little nervous tension, as he pulled another handful of soft crabs out of the float. The men were removing the soft crabs from the water as fast as they could. I remembered that if the soft crabs stay in the water too long after shedding, they would not remain soft. Take them out of the water and the shedding or hardening process stops.

*"They're sheddin' all at once!"*

*First Light*

After pulling a considerable amount of crabs from the floats, Nussie and Captain Harry carried as many as they could over to the bait shanty to quickly sort by size, place them in trays and refrigerate. This they repeated several times. Some of the crabs were set aside to be cleaned and frozen by the watermen's wives. Mesmerized, I stayed out of the way and watched.

At first light, Nussie changed tack and began to prepare the *Miss Julie* for another day of peeler potting. Johnny arrived to lend a hand. When all was ready, Nussie headed for the little skiff tied to the dock. He pulled the skiff around to the side of the floats that held the Jimmy (male) crabs. Once there, he netted several hard crabs. "Gotta attract the she crabs somehow," he said. Nussie placed the male crabs aboard the *Miss Julie*, and Johnny cast off the lines. Away we went. It was 5:45 a.m.

*The soft crabs were sorted by size and refrigerated.*

*Fishin' up some Jimmy's to attract the females*

We sailed toward the Holland Straits. (Even though we were in a powerboat and not in a sailboat, Nussie used the term "sail" when referring to going from here to there in his boat.) Our ride to the crabbing grounds was a little longer than it had been the previous fall. The Straits are about seven miles from Deal Island on the west side of Tangier Sound, between Bloodsworth and South Marsh Islands. As captain, it is Nussie's job to know where and when to set his crab pots. He makes the decisions and bears the risks.

The excitement of the early morning was still in the air. There was quiet anticipation as the men set up their equipment. The first crab pot was hooked and pulled in. A respectable half dozen or so, mostly she crabs. To my surprise, there were no jelly fish and the crab pots were as clean as new. The contents were dumped into the culling box and Johnny began to sort. The now empty pot was re-baited with a fresh Jimmy crab. Nussie told me, "Some of the Jimmy's get weak, some die. They have to be replaced with fresh ones."

*There were no jelly fish and the crab pots were clean and new and full of crabs.*

*A culling box
full of peelers*

All through this time and as on my previous trips, with intense concentration, Nussie was on the lookout for the next crab pot and almost instinctively maneuvered the *Miss Julie* to it. In came another pot with somewhat better results, perhaps a dozen or so. "That's pretty good," I thought.

Things really started to heat up when the next crab pot was pulled in, containing at least thirty crabs. "And they're mostly peelers," Johnny said with a big smile. "We're on 'em now." The next several crab pots were loaded with crabs. As before, Johnny did the culling while Nussie sailed to the next pot. This time though, so many crabs were being caught, the culling box still held crabs in it when we reached the next pot. Nussie pulled the throttle back, slowed the boat down a little and helped with the culling.

Johnny put a buster in the bucket of water so it would continue its shedding process. Something else was happening that caught my eye. Before Johnny and Nussie put the peelers in the peeler basket, they would break the top pincher part on both of the crab's claws. It was a subtle thing and it happened fast. I could hardly tell it was done by looking at the crab. Nussie explained, "We do that 'cuz they're easier to handle, they can't pinch each other and they don't eat each other in the floats when they shed out." Normally, the busters are transferred to the shedding box on the washboard after a run or row of crab pots are pulled. We left a buster in the bucket so I could occasionally take it out of the water to inspect it and photograph its advancement. It was amazing just how much bigger the new soft crab was, compared to the hard exoskeleton it came out of.

"We're on 'em now."

A buster in process

All morning long,
we caught crabs.

Every once in a while, two crabs (a male and a female) were still doubled up when the crab pot was pulled in. They didn't separate during the commotion of the crab pot getting pulled to the surface. The male was always on top and the female below. In some cases, the female had already shed into a soft crab and they were in the mating process. In others, the male stood over defending the female while waiting for her to shed.

In addition to the crabs, other species were pulled up in the pots. There were oyster toads, Hogchokers and an occasional jellyfish. The oyster toad is an ugly brown fish of no use or interest to fisherman. The Hogchokers were kind of cute with stripped, feathery fins and a smile on their faces, but were also of no use or interest. And of course, the jellyfish were just an annoyance. All were returned to the water unharmed.

Oyster Toad and Hogchockers

Nussie said he occasionally catches legal size flounder later in the season. "Now that's a good eatin' fish!" There were also undersized crabs. They, too, were returned to the water. I photographed the underside of a male and female crab in order to show their differences. Most interesting to me, some of the crabs that were caught were "different" from the others. One in particular had blue spots over its face, claws and underside. Another crab had the beginnings of new claws. As I was photographing, Nussie said, "They can grow their claws or legs back after losin' 'em in battle or during the shed." He continued, "I've caught a few with deformed claws, too."

The Sook (female) on the left; the Jimmy (male) on the right

*Captain Mike Webster sails past aboard the Queen Elizabeth.*

Captain Dickey's brother, Mike, sailed past aboard his boat, the *Queen Elizabeth*. He was working the same edge as Nussie. The two men exchanged a few good-natured remarks and went on about their business. We came to the county line where, once again, the line of crab pots abruptly ended. We made a turn and changed direction.

*The final tally – 13 bushels.*

As the morning started to heat up, Johnny covered the day's catch with whatever material he could find to keep the crabs out of the sun. All morning long, we caught crabs. Sometimes I counted half a dozen per pot, sometimes dozens. All told, we fished approximately 400 crab pots. The final tally was 13 bushels of crabs. It was a good day by anybody's standards. Nussie said his best day of the season was three days earlier when he caught 24 bushels of peelers.

It was easy to see why the floats back at Windsor's were loaded.

*Nussie's distinctively marked float*

# Ten

## Jimmy Crabs

As the spring doubler season run winds down, Nussie has less of a need to retain all the Jimmy crabs in his floats for baiting pots. It is then that he begins to sell Jimmy's at the commercial dock, or he keeps hold of them in his floats for future sales.

It was June and whenever possible, I found myself hanging out at Windsor's Marina, spending time with Nussie and Captain Harry. Their cheerful manner and laid back ways and their patient answers to my many questions kept me coming around.

One early afternoon I was sitting in the shanty passing the time of day when a customer pulled up. After the usual small talk, the guy asked, "Got any hard crabs?"

"How many you want?" Nussie replied.

*"Got any hard crabs?"*

"A bushel if you got'em." Nussie was up and walking to the dock where the hard crabs were kept. Once on the end of the dock, I could clearly see the vibrant blue claws of the Jimmy crabs. They sharply contrasted with the red claws of the Sooks (females) that had been my most recent photographic subjects.

The hard crabs were bunched up in the corners. One crab was eating the leg of another. "I guess they're hungry," I commented. Unlike the peelers in the floats, these crabs could still clamp down hard with their claws and do some damage, as their claws had not been clipped.

*Fishin' up some Jimmy's to eat*

Nussie began to net the crabs and dump them in a bushel basket. I remembered him telling me how important it was to break the claws of the peeler crabs. These Jimmy crabs were grabbing and pinching each other, the webbing of the net, the side of the basket and anything else they could get a hold of. As the basket started to fill, the crabs tried to crawl out. To stop them, Nussie placed a basket with the bottom cut out of it into the basket with the crabs. This allowed him to add more crabs to the original basket while raising the sides higher so the tasty critters couldn't crawl out.

*Beautiful Chesapeake Bay Blue Crabs*

I moved in for some close-up photos while staying out of the crabs' reach and Nussie's way. "They are some fine lookin' Jimmy crabs," I thought. The blues and greens were vibrant. They were feisty too! Talk about *fresh*.

When the basket was full, Nussie pulled the bottomless basket out and quickly put the lid on over the moving crabs. We all moseyed back to the shanty so the customer could settle up. Paid in full, he walked away happy with his bushel of live hard crabs. A crab feast in the making.

# Eleven

## Off to Market

*Full box of Primes ready for market*

A year had passed since I first met Captain Nussie Webster and Captain Harry Windsor and things were going quite well. My time spent at Windsor's Marina and aboard the *Miss Julie* had been enjoyable and I had captured some good images on film.

One hot August day, I arrived at Windsor's to go fishing. I found the men preparing their soft crabs for market. As usual, they worked as a team. Tray by tray, the soft crabs were pulled from the old refrigerators that had the shelves taken out. The crabs were then repacked according to size into plastic coated cardboard trays.

*Jumbo soft crabs – highly prized in restaurants*

The men patiently taught me the terms for the different sizes of crabs. The smallest crabs are called Meeds. A size up from Meeds are Hotels, then Primes and Jumbos. Finally, the largest are called Whales.

When a tray was full, a layer of white paper was placed on top of the crabs. After that, a layer of straw was spread out evenly over the white paper. Finally, a thin layer of crushed ice went on top. "Just enough ice to keep 'em cool," Captain Harry said. "Too much ice can kill 'em."

*"Just enough ice to keep 'em cool."*

KEEP REFRIGERATED
SOFT CRABS
PERISHABLE

THIS SIDE UP
THIS BOX CONTAINS LIVE SOFT
SHELL CRABS PLEASE HANDLE
WITH CARE. DON'T STAND ON
BOX—DON'T DROP

*Off to market*

Each tray was then stacked into a plastic-coated cardboard box, three trays per box. "These crabs 'll be in New York tonight," Nussie said as he loaded several boxes of soft crabs onto his pickup truck. We drove across the bridge and onto Deal Island. A quick right turn took us to Deal Island Harbor and Island Seafood, a seafood processor and middleman. Upon delivery, Nussie was paid right then and there for his crabs. In later years, Nussie would find some of his own buyers. Sometimes they are end users like a restaurant, sometimes a wholesaler. And then there are the occasional retail and bait sales.

My friends and I almost always get our fishin' bait from "The Nuss Man."

# Twelve

## Wingate Harbor

From Deal Island, by boat, the directions Tall Man had given me were: "Head west across Tangier Sound and into the Hooper Straits. On the right, you'll see Bishops Head Point. As you go through the Straits, head northwest into the Honga River while keepin' land in sight on yer norther side. The next point you come to is Crab Point." Very fitting, I thought. Tall Man went on, "Go past Crab Point and bear to the right into Duck Point Cove. Look for buoy #5. It'll mark the entrance to Wingit Harbor."

I had an urge to take some photographs. It was a late Sunday afternoon when I reached buoy # 5 in my boat, the *Cash Flow*. The ride over from Deal Island was smooth. The weather was good and the directions Tall Man had given me were spot on. A large osprey nest sat atop the buoy. It was good to see the birds doing so well and building nests throughout the Bay area. The mast of a Skipjack was visible in the distance, telling me I was in the right place.

*Buoy #5 clearly marked*
*Wingate Harbor.*
*The resident osprey must*
*have been out fishing.*

*Wilma Lee*

*Wingate Harbor*

*A day off for the Bonnie Rose*

As I motored closer and entered the harbor, I saw the Skipjack was the *Wilma Lee*, resting quietly for the summer. On the southeast side of the harbor was a large white building that housed a crab-picking operation. On the northwest side of the harbor, several workboats were lined up side by side along the bulkhead, all moored bow in. An occasional pleasure boat mixed with the workboats. About halfway down the row of workboats, I found the *Bonnie Rose*, taking the day off. The sky was unusually clear blue with puffy white clouds, the water was calm, and the lighting was perfect for a few pictures. I went to work.

# *Thirteen*

## Trotlining with Tall Man

*"This is what we're goin' after."*

I t was 4:30 a.m. and still dark when I returned to Wingate Harbor the morning of July 3rd. A full moon was nearing the end of its journey across the night sky. Tall Man pulled up in his pickup truck. "Good mornin'," he said with conviction and sincerity. He must have had everything ready because he immediately headed for the *Bonnie Rose* and added, "The crabs are waitin'. Let's git goin'."

He fired up his boat, untied the ropes and off we went, the dark of night still upon us. As we left the safety of the harbor, Tall Man announced, "It's a little breezy this mornin', so we're goin' to go a little further than usual. The wind's out o' the west. We'll git real close to Hoopers Island and use it to block the wind." Tall Man left the helm near the stern and we walked to the cabin to settle in for the ride. Our conversation quickly turned to crabbing. "I love crabbin'," he said. "Can't wait to get goin' in the mornin'. There's nothin' better than a sunrise on the water." We were quiet for awhile, just listening to the hum of the motor and enjoying the ride.

About halfway to our destination, he said, "I usually set up here near the middle of the Honga River, but as you can see, it wouldn't be too good today." The water looked choppy, but with the size of the *Bonnie Rose* and from the seat I was in, I had hardly noticed.

"I've seen worse." I said.

Tall Man responded, "It's the crabs that don't like it rough. They let go of the bait if they feel the slightest movement." Twenty minutes passed before Tall Man pulled back on the throttle and headed to the back of the boat. I followed. The first light of day arrived as Tall Man set his first trotline.

"That doesn't look like eel," I said in reference to the bait tied to the line in five-foot intervals. "I had always heard the bait of choice for trotliners was eel."

"It used to be," he responded while he worked. "We now use bull lips."

"Bull lips?" I asked.

"Yep. They're cheaper than eel and stay on the line a lot longer. They're tough as leather."

73

*It was a gorgeous morning.*

Tall Man said the line was 1,000 feet long. When it was all set, we headed back to the beginning of the line. Then Tall Man pulled out a custom-made wooden contraption that he attached to the washboard next to the spot from which he piloted the boat. It was designed to hang over the water and allow the trotline to run through it while supporting the crabber's net. By this time, the morning sun edged over the horizon to the east and began to light the day as the full moon was setting in the west. What a way to start the day! It was a gorgeous morning and we both acknowledged the moment. I fully understood and agreed with him. There truly is nothing better than a sunrise on the Bay.

*Number one Jimmy's go into one basket and number two's go into the other. The undersized go back over the side.*

*Tall Man makes his first run of the day.*

Tall Man began his first run down the line. "I'll only set one line for now. We'll see if this spot pans out before I set the other."

Within minutes of the first run down the line, the culling box began to fill up with big, blue-clawed Jimmy crabs. There were a few red tips (females) caught, but not many. When the culling box was close to full, Tall Man throttled the engine back and dropped the *Bonnie Rose* into neutral. He then walked forward to the culling box and began to sort the crabs by size. The number one Jimmy's went into one basket, the number two's into another, and the undersized went back over the side. Noticeably absent were the peelers. Then I remembered Nussie telling me that when a crab gets close to shedding, it stops eating. That's why we weren't catching any peelers. I was beginning to understand the difference between fishing for hard crabs and fishing for peelers.

Up to that point, Tall Man had been talking with his buddies on the radio, but now, the Captain of the *Maurice* stopped by for a chat. The conversation centered on who was catching the crabs and where. Tall Man mentioned that he was doing pretty well so far. By the time we finished up the first run, we had over two bushels of beautiful hard crabs. Not a bad start.

It was now time for Tall Man to set his second line but there was something else to consider. I was told that the Captain of the *Gloria B* had his lines run in the same area. So when he maneuvered close enough to talk with her captain in person, Tall Man asked if it would be OK to run his second line nearby. "Sure," came the reply. After we moved on to do so, Tall Man said to me, "It's nice to be polite."

*There is always time to see who is catching the crabs and where.*

Tall Man set the second line and made a couple of runs. He had to stop every so often to cull his catch. Things were looking good as the crabs were cooperating. I could see some of them let go of the bait as they approached the surface, at which point Tall Man skillfully made a move with his dip net to scoop them up. Very few avoided capture if they held on long enough to be seen from above.

The water rushed through the metal dip net as the boat moved forward.

The sun was getting higher and the light was perfect for taking pictures. The water rushed through the metal dip net as the boat moved forward. Sometimes there were as many as a dozen crabs in the net before Tall Man emptied it into the culling box. It was a wonderful sight to see those crabs coming in.

By the end of the third run, the numbers had dwindled and Tall Man decided to make a move. He maneuvered his boat to the large black plastic jug he used to mark the end of the line. When he got close enough, he grabbed the line with his boat hook and pulled in the weighted end. It was a big piece of old chain. He put the end of the line with the chain in a large white barrel and wrapped the line around a winder. "One thousand feet is a lot of line to pull in by hand," he said. He pulled a lever and in came the trotline. This procedure was repeated with the second trotline. It was mid-morning by the time Tall Man had moved a little further north and reset his trotlines.

*Sorting Jimmy's by size can be painful
even while wearing heavy gloves.*

The day turned out to be magnificent. With not a cloud in the sky, the vivid blue background provided excellent conditions for taking pictures. Tall Man made a few more runs down his trotlines, netting some crabs and culling. I clicked off several more exposures. The catch was still abundant, but not quite like it had been on our earlier runs.

*Heavily armed, this Jimmy was ready for a fight.*

It was late morning when Tall Man called it a day. The final tally was eleven bushels. Both lines were pulled in with the winder, same as before, and we headed for the harbor. Before we left, Tall Man had another conversation with the men aboard the *Gloria B*, where each captain reported on the day's catch.

*Calling it a day, Tall Man lets his winder do the work.*

*Tools of the trade*

During our voyage back to the harbor, Tall Man skippered the *Bonnie Rose* from the stern of the boat instead of the cabin. From there, he was able to go over each trotline and re-bait them with new bull lips where necessary. After the lines were re-baited, each line was fed entirely into a different barrel with a liquid that preserved the bull lips and prevented them from deteriorating. "This way, I'm all ready to go in the mornin'," he said.

*Rebaiting trotlines in preparation of the next day's work.*

*Bull lips, the preferred bait of trotliners.*

We reached the harbor and headed for the commercial dock where the crab picking operation was located. Tall Man unloaded and sold the day's catch. He then refueled the *Bonnie Rose*. No wonder Tall Man was ready to go first thing in the morning. All the prep work is done the day before.

*Back at the dock, the day's catch is sold.*

# *Fourteen*

## Deal Island Harbor

*Deal Island Harbor*

I was on my way back from Wenona Harbor where I had been photographing Captain Dicky's Skipjack, the *Caleb W. Jones*, when I decided to document Deal Island Harbor with film and camera. I didn't know why but it just felt right at the time. It wasn't until many years later that I understood what was behind the constant urge to photograph and record the area on film.

Similar to Wenona and Wingate Harbors, the tall masts of Skipjacks towering above all else could be seen from a distance. As I drove closer to Deal Island, Island Seafood, housed in a large white building, came into view.

Approaching from west to east, channel markers and buoys designate the channel and the entrance to the harbor. Rock jetties reach out from both sides of the entrance to protect the harbor from storms.

*Island Seafood*

*Billy Anderson's original shanty
and the Miss Teresa*

Just inside the breakwater on the right, a new oyster research facility for The Department of Natural Resources was being constructed. Moored next to this facility was the *Wasp*, a boat owned by C.J. Longenfeller and used for his shell planting operation. Further east is Island Seafood. Next to it, two Skipjacks moored side by side, their tall masts reaching to a beautiful blue sky. Around the harbor after Island Seafood is the county boat ramp. On the other side of the ramp, about fifteen boat slips. The Department of Natural Resources has the first two slips for their police boats. Then there is an old country store and gas dock. Finally, just before the Deal Island Bridge is a waterman's shanty and crab shedding operation owned by Billy Anderson, a friend of Nussie's.

*The Wasp*

Situated on the left side of the breakwater as you enter Deal Island Harbor, a substantial white sand bar stands out. On the north side of the sand bar was a place called Last Chance Marina, which is now dilapidated and half filled with sand. At that time, about twelve watermen docked their boats there. Overlooking Last Chance Marina was an old restaurant. Following along the shoreline on the left before the bridge, a small gut, a narrow body of water, leads to Scotts Cove Marina, the largest commercial and recreational marina in the Deal Island area. After the gut is Deal Island Bridge. To get to Windsor's Marina by boat, you go under the rickety bridge and bear to the left.

*Scotts Cove Marina*

*The old, rickety
Deal Island Bridge*

As many times as I had sailed in and out of Deal Island Harbor, I had previously taken it for granted. Growing up, it was just a place where my father launched his boat to take my brothers and me fishing, period. But now, the entire area was becoming more to me. The more time I spend here, the more I realize that this is truly a special place. Unique and beautiful, the entire area is a window in time, where rich nautical tradition abounds. This is a place where the ways of the Chesapeake Bay Watermen have remained relatively unchanged for generations, until just recently.

# Fifteen

## Scraping with Brother Stevie

*Captain Stevie and the Miss Kelly*

My good luck with the watermen continued when I learned that Nussie had a brother and that his brother was a crab scraper. One of the mornings we were sailing out of Deal Island Harbor, Nussie casually mentioned that the guy in the boat we were passing was his brother, Stevie. I commented on how low Stevie's boat, the *Miss Kelly*, sat in the water. Nussie explained Stevie is a crab scraper, and the boat needs to be low to the water for this kind of work. "Ah, another photographic opportunity," I thought to myself. Lots of people have heard of trotlining and crab potting, but very few, including me, knew anything about crab scraping. Nussie gave me Stevie's phone number. I called him the next day.

"I leave real early in the morning!" was Stevie's spirited response to my request when we spoke.

"That won't be a problem," I told him.

*It was pitch dark and breezy when we began our journey across Tangier Sound.*

It was still pitch dark and a little breezy the morning I met up with Captain Stevie Webster to go crab scraping. With no idea what to expect, I jumped aboard the *Miss Kelly* with my camera equipment, a sandwich and a few soft drinks. Stevie untied his lines and off we sailed. "The wind is blowin' purdy strong out 'a the west, so we're goin' east through the thoroughfare and use Deal Island as a wind block."

At the very last minute, he changed his mind and headed west out of the harbor. As soon as we left the protection of the rock jetty at the entrance of the harbor, the wind and the accompanying waves hitting the boat made for a bumpy ride. Since the *Miss Kelly* sat so low in the water, waves started crashing over the gunnels.

The wet ride didn't faze Stevie, since he had on oil skins to protect him. As for me, I huddled close to the cabin for protection from the onslaught of the incoming deluge, which I could not see as it was still dark. After riding like that for awhile, Stevie left the stern and headed for the helm in the dry cabin. I quickly followed.

Once in the channel, ever larger waves were breaking over the side of the boat as we headed west toward the islands. I felt vulnerable, in fact, more at risk than at any other time I had been aboard the crab boats. I wondered if Stevie was testing me. The fact that the *Miss Kelly* sat so low in the water made it seem rougher than it probably was. This rough sea in Nussie's or Tall Man's boats would have been much safer and less threatening.

*The Miss Kelly's stern tiller*

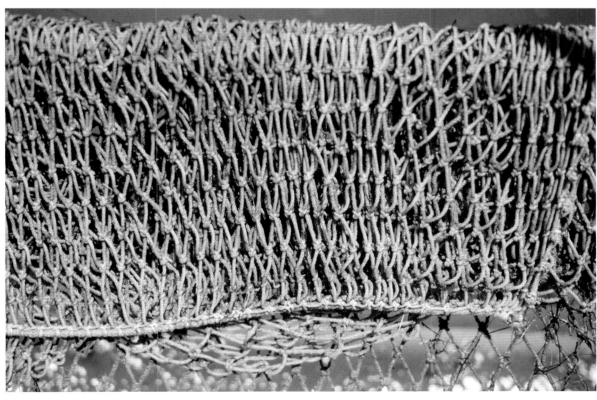

*The large meshed net is fastened to a metal frame.*

As Stevie had calculated, the water calmed as we got close to his destination, the east side of South Marsh Island. It was still dark when Stevie dropped his crab scraper over the side. The scraper reminded me of an oyster dredge in size and shape but it had no teeth. In place of teeth, a flat bar was used so the Bay grasses are not pulled up by the roots. The idea is that the grass breaks or cuts off, like mowing the backyard with a lawnmower. Instead of a metal cage to hold oysters, there was a long meshed net or bag to catch the crabs. A heavy rope, about the same size as one used on an oyster dredge, secured the scraper to the stern of the boat. The process was simple enough. Drop the scraper over the side in fairly shallow water and slowly pull it along the bottom with the *Miss Kelly* to "scrape up" the crabs.

*Stevie slides the peelers into a compartmentalized wooden box partially filled with bay water.*

*The culling process was similar to Nussie's. Each crab was inspected for signs and sorted accordingly.*

The sun began to creep up over the horizon to the east when Stevie stopped the boat and pulled in the scraper for the first time. Along with some bay grass, in came crabs in different stages of molting and shedding. There were soft crabs, peelers, a few hard crabs and of course, a few jellyfish. The culling process was similar to Nussie's. Stevie inspected each hard crab for signs. The peelers were placed into a compartmentalized wooden box partially filled with bay water. "I sectioned off the box to keep the water from sloshing around and to sort the crabs according to how soon they'll be sheddin'," said Stevie. The soft crabs were placed on a tray and covered with a wet burlap bag.

*Soft crabs*

Previously, Nussie told me that the ratio of hard crabs to peeler crabs to soft crabs changes depending on what phase of the run the crabs were in. Sometimes, early in the run, there are no soft crabs. Later in the run, the percentage of soft crabs is usually much higher. He also said he thinks the most important factors at the start of the season and each run are water temperature and the cycle of the moon.

*The Miss Kelly was still moving when Captain Stevie pulls in the scraper by hand.*

Surprisingly, when Stevie pulled the scraper in for the second time, I recalled those early childhood trips with my father when we went looking for soft crabs to net while wading in the crystal clear water. This was a similar place. It might even have been the same place. But there was a significant difference. The water is no longer crystal clear, but instead, downright opaque. The scrape muddied it even more.

Unlike Nussie, Stevie was going after soft crabs in addition to peelers. Stevie said, "I think the crabs go to the grassy shallows to hide when they're sheddin' into soft crabs." This made me realize that the biggest difference between scraping and peeler potting was that Stevie and the other scrapers catch soft crabs after they shed out in the wild. This would be rare for Nussie and the other peeler potters who work in the deeper water.

*The Miss Myrt*

*The Miss Ashley*

As the morning progressed, the weather improved. The winds moderated and the clouds just about disappeared, leaving a beautiful blue background with a few traces of white. A few other watermen worked the area. With their boats, the *Miss Ashley* and the *Miss Myrt*, they pulled their scrapes along the bottom, same as Stevie.

I was starting to wear down when Stevie finally called it quits. I'd almost bet he stayed out longer than usual to test me further. The ride back to the harbor was smooth, as Tangier Sound was now flat calm. Or, "slick cam" as the watermen say. Stevie cleaned up his boat as we sailed across. He pulled up to Island Seafood to unload and sell his crabs. Since he did not shed crabs, he sold his entire catch then and there.

Back at the dock I thanked Stevie for allowing me to accompany him and headed for home.

I later recounted my experience to Nussie and mentioned the uneasy feeling the incident gave me. Nussie said, "The *Miss Kelly*, as other boats do, often leaks." To tease me a little more, he asked if I wore a life preserver. "You were puttin' yer life in Stevie's hands." He grinned.

"I'm glad I didn't know that before I sailed aboard 'er," I retorted.

*Captain Stevie Webster*

# Sixteen

## Workin' Alone

*Workin' alone*

As the peeler season neared its end, I decided to go out once more and catch up with Captain Nussie while he fished for crabs. I found him working alone. "That's a first," I thought to myself. "Where's Johnny?" I asked. Nussie shrugged his shoulders with an "I have no idea" motion.

I was on my own in my boat, the *Cash Flow*. I pulled out my camera and went to work. It didn't take me long to realize that, by myself, this would be no easy task. Piloting my boat while photographing Nussie aboard the *Miss Julie* was challenging, to say the least. Because I needed to get up close, there was little room for error. I had only seconds to snap a picture or two before getting back to the helm and making an adjustment to the *Cash Flow*. Fortunately, the wind was calm and so was Tangier Sound, so my boat stayed relatively steady. I have learned over time that it is quite a challenge to take a photograph from a moving boat while keeping the horizon line level. Add in the wind factor and rough seas, taking photographs from a moving boat gets even more demanding.

Nussie did the job of two men as he piloted his boat from pot to pot. He hooked the crab pot line and buoy with his boat hook as he passed, while continuing to steer the *Miss Julie* toward the next pot. He did so as he throttled the boat's speed down and wrapped the line around the winder. He then pushed a lever on the winder and in came the crab pot. There was some serious wear on the side of the *Miss Julie*. This happens because the pots actually scrape against the hull as they are hauled in. Similar to the previous August, there was a large amount of growth on the pots and just a few crabs caught. But the biggest difference this time was that Nussie had to open the pots and shake the crabs out by himself, a real upper body workout. I left Nussie as I found him, late in the season, catching a few more crabs.

Not only is Captain Nussie one of the first to start peeler potting in the spring, he is one of the last to end in the fall. This late in the season, most of the other watermen are preparing for the fall oyster season and Tangier Sound is no longer covered with crab pot floats. In Maryland, only the commercial crabbers who use crab pots to catch hard crabs work later into the fall and early winter.

*Shaking the crabs out of the crabpot, Nussie gets an upper body workout.*

104

*I left Nussie as I found him, late in the season, catching a few more crabs.*

There is a downside to crab potting late in the season, a time of year when there is more financial risk for the watermen. Hurricanes frequent the east coast and their powerful winds and accompanying waves can wipe out a waterman's inventory of crab pots. When this happens, it costs thousands of dollars to replace them. Choices have to be made weighing the risks of possibly losing equipment from a storm and losing income from crabs not caught when the pots are pulled from the water. It is not unusual for Nussie to make a mad dash to collect his entire supply of crab pots when he feels a big storm approaching. That year, Nussie was lucky. Most of his pots were already out of the water by the time Hurricane Gloria headed toward the Delmarva Peninsula and Chesapeake Bay. When Gloria moved closer, Nussie pulled his remaining pots and had the *Miss Julie* hauled up on the bank at Scotts Cove for protection from the storm. I loaded the *Cash Flow* onto her trailer and fastened the rig to a large tree behind the big white house at Windsor's Marina.

It was several days after the storm before I made my way back. I had tried to get there sooner, but fallen trees across Deal Island Road blocked my way. At Windsor's, I discovered that, considering the strength of the storm, everybody had made out fairly well. The worst of it was the power outage due to several downed utility lines. Nussie maintained a generator to keep his freezers running and his crabs from thawing. Nussie and I talked for a while. He recounted how high the water reached at the height of the storm surge. "It was over the docks AND the bulkhead a right good ways," he said.

In the fall, it's about fish bait too. Trout fishing in Tangier Sound usually heats up just as the soft crab season winds down. As the fishing gets better, the peelers and soft crabs, bait of choice, get scarce. They become a hot commodity and the price goes up. Conversely, during the doubler season, when the peeler crab harvest peaks, seemingly everybody has soft crabs and the price is driven down. Supply and demand.

*Fishin' at Bogz*

# Seventeen

## Final Stages of the Shed

When I reached the float, a peeler crab was nearing the final stages of its shedding process. It was what Nussie calls a "buster." I turned off the water in the float to see the buster more clearly. At first glance, the crab looked dead. I recalled Nussie telling me that many crabs get "hung up" in the shedding process and die. The bigger they get, the harder it is for them to shed.

Then, a movement, hardly perceptible at first, but it was there. I continued to watch. There it was again – another movement. The crab was trying to pull away from its old shell. Little by little, leg by leg, the crab wiggled and wrestled its way out of its shell that looked about two sizes too small. The claws were the last to come out and the newly formed soft crab was free at last. The crab appeared weak and hardly moved for several minutes. After it regained its strength, Nussie came by and fished it up. That is what I call a fresh soft crab!

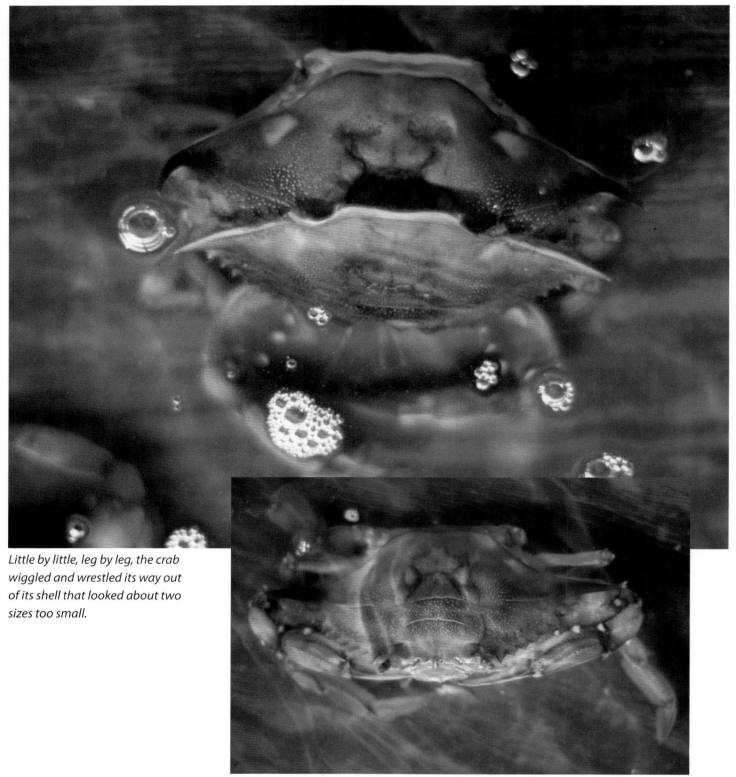

*Little by little, leg by leg, the crab wiggled and wrestled its way out of its shell that looked about two sizes too small.*

*Just shed out – a FRESH softcrab*

"It's no wonder that the female crabs double up under the male crabs for protection while shedding," I thought. New soft crabs are totally defenseless. Amazingly, the male crabs and juvenile females generally survive on their own. Watching the transformation of the peeler crab shedding into a soft crab was a remarkable learning experience, and gave me a deep appreciation of the tenacious Chesapeake Bay blue crab.

# Eighteen

## Dry Docked

Wooden workboats, and for that matter any workboats, require a lot of maintenance. Life on Chesapeake Bay, the wear and tear of the salt water, the sun and crab pots scraping up the sides, all take their toll. To properly maintain their most important tool of the trade, every year the watermen have their boats lifted out of the water and put up on dry dock to be scraped and painted. For Nussie, this takes place at the end of the crabbing season at Scotts Cove Marina. Sometimes the watermen do this work themselves; sometimes they pay to have it done.

Junior and Jack Willing are brothers who have owned and operated the marina for years. I had spent many hours with them the previous year while they rebuilt the *Caleb W. Jones*, Captain Dicky Webster's working Skipjack.

With prior arrangements made, Nussie's crabbing boat, the *Miss Julie*, was "hauled up on the bank," as Nussie would say.

One or the other of the brothers positioned the *Miss Julie* on the travel lift, raised it out of the water, and placed it on large wooden blocks up on land. The boat was then left to dry out before it was scraped, sanded and repainted. Beautiful and ready for next season, it's then returned to the water.

*End of the season*

*All painted up*

# Nineteen

## Captain Harry Windsor

Mooring the boat at Windsor's was working out well, and I was spending more and more time with the watermen. Photographing the watermen's way of life had become one of my favorite hobbies. More opportunities for taking pictures made for better results. Moreover, Captain Harry and Nussie kept an eye on my boat for me. I had never left my rig in the water for an extended period of time before. Having it moored at Windsor's made me feel as secure as I felt with the boat safe and sound in my own driveway. Plus, Captain Harry was always a wealth of information when it came to where and when the fish were biting and what bait to use to catch them. And, most of the bait I needed for fishing – soft crab – was right there! I looked forward to our visits as much as the actual fishing trips.

One afternoon, Captain Harry showed me a copy of *National Fisherman Magazine* that contained an article about a photo contest. "Why don't 'cha give it a try?" he suggested.

"No reason not to," I said. So I entered a few photographs of Nussie at work aboard the *Miss Julie*. To my surprise, a few months later, I arrived at Windsor's to find Captain Harry with a more recent copy of *National Fisherman*.

With a big smile, Captain Harry handed the magazine to me and said, "Ya' made it!" There he was, Captain Nussie Webster, working his crab pots in a national publication. Captain Harry was so proud to see his grandson in the magazine.

On another visit, I was preparing to head out to the fishing grounds, excited to get out on the water. It was a perfect day for fishing – bright and clear, not too hot, not too cold, and not much wind. It was customary to chat with Captain Harry at the shanty for a bit while getting bait. As I did so, he noticed I was rushing around and seemed to be in a hurry. "Sloooow down," he told me. "No need to hurry when yer down here."

This attitude is one of the many aspects of the life these watermen lead that I find so appealing. No hurry, no problem. There is always time to talk. I always remember that advice and try to remind myself of it when I do get in a rush. Heading to Deal Island to go fishing is no time to be in a hurry. Over the years, I have found that it's the journey and anticipation of the journey, not the final destination, that is most rewarding.

I frequently wished I had a tape recorder running as Captain Harry talked about the "old days" or the ways of the crab. But I decided not to use one. I didn't want it to influence our easy conversations. And Captain Harry was too sharp for me to sneak one in without his knowledge.

I will never forget the time Captain Harry invited me to go fishing with him. I was a little taken aback when he offered, quite honored he had asked. We had come a long way in our friendship during my many visits. My time spent in the shanty talking and asking questions was always enjoyable and always informative. This man was very likable and full of knowledge and experience! The ways of the Chesapeake Bay watermen were in his blood. Additionally, his accumulated familiarity with the history of the area was profound.

We left Windsor's on a beautiful October morning a little after dawn. We sailed aboard Captain Harry's tri-hull powered by an old but reliable Evenrude outboard. This time of year, he moored the boat in the spot at Windsor's where Nussie unloaded his catch during the spring doubler run. When we reached the place Captain Harry called Bogz, he dropped anchor. We prepared our fishing gear, and as Captain Harry was cutting up some soft crabs for bait, he repeated something he had said before. "There's nothin' better to fish with than a fresh piece 'a soft crab." More than once during our discussions in the shanty, talk centered around bait and tackle choices. Our mutual friend, Don Fountain, had started to use beads and spoons on his hooks in an effort to attract more fish and swore by them. Captain Harry called all that stuff "jewelry" and would always swear by soft crab.

When all was ready, we dropped our lines. I thought I knew a little about fishing, but Captain Harry really had the touch. We were fishing about four feet apart but it might as well have been a mile. He caught eighteen trout to my three. I felt like a novice. Each time Captain Harry caught a trout, he would land it in one fluid motion from the water to a bushel basket sitting on the floor of the boat. No nets were used. If by chance a fish got away, that was a risk he was willing to take, but it didn't happen often. To add insult to injury, each time he dropped his line down into the water, he would announce "My turn," as though I was the one catching all the fish! He did so with a wily little grin. In two and a half hours, we were done and on our way back to Windsor's. We didn't fish for long that day. Pretty standard for Captain Harry. He didn't stay too long on any fishing trip.

*"My turn."*

*Each time Captain Harry caught a trout,
he would land it in one fluid motion
from the water to the bushel basket.*

*Windor's Marina*

On another occasion, my fishing buddies Jim Coffman and Don Fountain were with me when I showed up at Windsor's looking for some bait to fish with for the second day in a row. We had an extraordinary fishing trip the previous evening so we were wound up. Much to our satisfaction, we had caught a mess of speckled trout. One of the most sought after game fish in Chesapeake Bay, speckled trout are also a first-rate fish to eat. Since it was customary to report on our fishing expeditions at the shanty, we gave an account to Captain Harry and Nussie and proclaimed our expectations of repeating this accomplishment that night. "Boys," Captain Harry said, "Ya've already caught those fish. Ya expect to do the same tonight?"

"No doubt," we each replied eagerly. We went on to recap the predicted weather and tides and announced that the time of day and conditions were the same as the previous night. Captain Harry just smiled and wished us luck. Needless to say, we didn't repeat the exceptional catch of the preceding day. We didn't even come close. Somehow, Captain Harry knew the odds were against us to duplicate the previous day's success before we even set out from the marina.

A different fine day, I arrived at Windsor's Marina around 3:00 o'clock in the afternoon. I wanted to learn more about Captain Harry Windsor. I found Captain Harry in his favorite chair in the shanty overlooking the harbor. When asked about his family, Captain Harry spoke of his father and grandfather. "They were both watermen, like me," he quietly said. He went back to the days when his grandfather owned a Skipjack. "It was pretty rough in those days. Oyster wars. Sometimes it was a violent life with shootin' and all. Durin' that time, we were the only marina with a boat railway in the area. My father did the work on the boats that needed repair."

He spoke of the disease that almost killed him in 1960. "Everybody thought it was cancer. I had severe weight loss and found out my food intake was turnin' to fat with no benefit to me. It was doin' me no good to eat. My doctors put me on some medicine and I retired and sold the marina. The buyers were two drunks from, I think, Philadelphia. Anyway, I moved to southeastern Florida and steadily got worse. Six months passed. Feelin' terrible and very unhappy, I decided that if I was gonna die, I might as well die at home, in Chance. When I returned, my luck changed. The doctors found a medication that allowed me to absorb the necessary nutrients from food. It took three long years to get my strength back, slowly buildin' up."

Captain Harry switched back to the subject of his family. "One of my sons loves the water. He's a sheriff in Dade County, Florida. He owns the marina and house now." (I had assumed Captain Harry's son bought it back from the northerners from Philadelphia, but I didn't ask.) "The other two could care less about the water."

"Sometimes I wish I could go back fifty or sixty years fer just one day and walk through the community. White picket fences in every yard with a hog out back. There were only two or three cars in the area back then and one belonged to the doctor."

His reminiscing continued. "When I got married, we drove to Princess Anne to the Justice of the Peace by horse and buggy. Back then, when ya got married, ya knew it was fer life. That was almost fifty years ago. I have twenty-eight grandchildren now," he proudly declared. After another pause and a look of yearning, he added, "I wish Nussie was of age and interested in crabbin' when I sold the marina."

I got his point.

Our conversation turned back to fishing. Captain Harry said, "I ran fishin' parties fer near 'bout twenty-five years. There's one party I'll always remember. Was about twenty years ago, back when our boats weren't all that fast. We were way down to Piney Island steady pullin' in trout. I could see a storm to the west and told the guys we had to leave. Well, they were havin' so much fun catchin' fish, they asked to stay fer a little longer. Against my better judgment, we stayed a bit. By the time we finally reached the harbor and land, they were kissin' the ground. 'Captain Harry. Next time ya say it's time to go, IT'S TIME TO GO!' they said." He chuckled.

He went on to tell me about the places they found rockfish forty years ago and how abundant they were only five or ten years back. "I believe it's overfishin' and new technology that's hurt fishin' the most. Pollution has had a negative effect, too."

"When I was still going out, fishin' the pots, I couldn't wait to get to the first pot, but I was glad when the last one was done." Captain Harry paused for a moment and continued. "I'm partners with Nussie now. He does the hard work. Ya know, it takes years of experience to learn the ways of the peeler crab."

Concluding with how he felt about his way of life he said, "I wouldn't recommend it to anybody. But if I had it to do over again, I wouldn't change a thing."

*Captain Harry Windsor – "I wouldn't recommend it to anybody.
But if I had it to do over again, I wouldn't change a thing."*

# Twenty

## Over the Years

*The largest trout I ever caught – 27 inches long, 8 pounds, 8 ounces.*

As I got busy with my career as a Realtor and with family, time spent with my watermen friends fell off. Luckily for me, I can still find a little time to go fishing.

I remember one September afternoon when Nussie and I sailed out of Windsor's Marina aboard the *Miss Julie* to fish for trout. This was before the days most folks had a GPS system to mark their favorite fishing spots. Back then, Nussie and Captain Harry would use a depth finder to locate the desired depth. Then they would line up a buoy with specific trees on land, or a particular house or church steeple, or a point of land to mark their favorite spots.

On this particular trip, we were fishing at Captain Harry's preferred spot, Bogz, catching some trout and having a good time. The flood tide had been pulling hard the entire time we were fishing. As evening approached and the tide finally started to go slack, Nussie made a move. "Let's try the deep over there in the channel," he said, as he fired up the *Miss Julie*. He moved the boat over a bit and we re-anchored. After only a short time, the breeze fell out to nothing and the tide went totally slack. We dropped our lines to seventy feet and within minutes we both had yellow fin trout (weakfish) on our lines. I hooked a big one that was actually pulling the boat sideways. When I finally landed the fish, I instantly realized it was the largest trout I had ever caught – and most likely ever will catch.

*The Miss Julie II moored at Windsor's*

Recalling that trip, I am reminded of a phone call I received at my office one afternoon. The caller identified himself as "Robert." At the time, I couldn't think of anybody I was working with by that name.

"Robert who?" I asked.

"Webster," was the caller's reply.

"Ah, Nussie, I've never heard you called Robert in all the years I've known you."

Nussie in as much ignored my observation and told me that the fishing was getting good and to come on down.

On another sunny afternoon, Nussie and I were sitting around the shanty when I asked, "Where did you get the nickname "Nussie" from?"

"My grandmother called me Nussie and I've been called Nussie ever since. That's 'bout it," he explained. It was as simple as that, no particular reason other than a grandmother's whim.

"How do you spell Nussie?" I asked.

"I don't know, man, I ain't never seen it spelled."

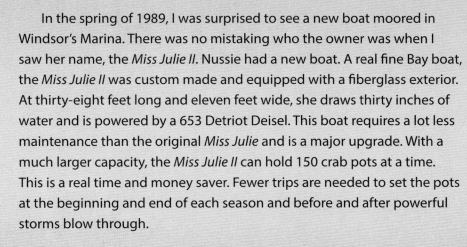

In the spring of 1989, I was surprised to see a new boat moored in Windsor's Marina. There was no mistaking who the owner was when I saw her name, the *Miss Julie II*. Nussie had a new boat. A real fine Bay boat, the *Miss Julie II* was custom made and equipped with a fiberglass exterior. At thirty-eight feet long and eleven feet wide, she draws thirty inches of water and is powered by a 653 Detriot Deisel. This boat requires a lot less maintenance than the original *Miss Julie* and is a major upgrade. With a much larger capacity, the *Miss Julie II* can hold 150 crab pots at a time. This is a real time and money saver. Fewer trips are needed to set the pots at the beginning and end of each season and before and after powerful storms blow through.

*Captain Nussie gearin' up for oysterin' aboard the Miss Julie II.*

*The Miss Julie II can hold 150 crab pots.*

In addition, shaft tonging for oysters is now a thing of the past for Nussie. At the end of crabbing season in the fall, the *Miss Julie II* is rigged for the winter oyster season with a patent tonging rig. Much more energy efficient and effective, this is a huge improvement from the old method of shaft tonging. The hardest, heaviest work is now done with hydraulics. The metal cage that scoops the oysters up off the bottom is larger and subsequently, so is the amount of oysters caught (if there are oysters to catch).

A notable example of Nussie's dry humor was demonstrated on a day Nussie, Steve Eccleston and I were fishing aboard the *Miss Julie II*. Steve spotted a bird high in the sky. It seemed to be about a mile away and looked like a dot. When Steve confidently identified the species of bird, Nussie and I looked at each other and back up at the bird. Out of the blue, Nussie said to Steve, "Ain't nothin' wrong with your eyes."

When I got the news that Captain Harry had passed away, I was saddened by the loss of a good friend. Additionally, it felt like his death signified an end of an era for me. I will surely miss our friendship and our talks together in that old shanty.

Shortly after Captain Harry's passing, and with my assistance, Nussie's uncle sold Windsor's Marina and the family chain of ownership was broken. It went unsaid, but I am sure it hurt Nussie a bit. Afterward, Nussie made a move and set up shop in Scotts Cove Marina, and has been there ever since.

One day I arrived at Scotts Cove to find a new name on what was formerly called The *Miss Julie II*. Nussie's boat had been re-named the *DUSTLA*. Nussie's children are Dustin and Lauren and the waterman tradition of naming their boats after their children is continued with this change.

Over the years, Scotts Cove Marina has seen its share of changes. Junior Willing passed away and handed down his share of the business to his son. The marina is now owned and run by his brother, Jack, and Junior's son, Eldon III. Junior's grandson, Shawn Messick, built a large metal building on the property to run a business painting and repairing boats. Jack and Eldon have made some major upgrades to the bulkheads, docks, boat yard and buildings. When I asked about Nussie renting space from them at the marina, Eldon thoughtfully said, "Nussie's a good person. A hard workin' fella that keeps his place neat and clean. He's an honest and talented person, too." In a different conversation I had with Jack, he added, "Nussie is easy goin' and anything you need him to do, he'll do it. He helps lots of people with their boats. He's a good carpenter, too."

*The Miss Julie II has a new name – DUSTLA.*

*The new Deal Island bridge*

Nussie's friend, Billy Anderson, has also been busy on the other side of Deal Island Harbor. His shanty and operation have seen some nice improvements as well. The Last Chance Marina closed and is now in shambles. The restaurant is gone and a large portion of the marina is silted in. The new Deal Island Bridge was completed and crossing over to the island has never been safer.

Nussie is continually looking for ways to improve his business. For example, the rather large building (I can't seem to bring myself around to calling it a shanty anymore) he built that houses his crab shedding floats can now be fully enclosed. Nussie covers the windows when needed to help regulate the water temperature. This increases the success rate of the peeler crabs shedding out into soft crabs.

Because of dwindling crab harvests and an oyster industry that is hanging on by a thread, many watermen have to supplement their incomes by means other than working on the water. For Nussie, that consists of carpentry work during the coldest months of the year. The sturdy house he built for himself is testament to his carpentry skills. He has also developed a bait business in which he sells live spot fish to bait and tackle shops, charter boat captains and other middlemen from Ocean City, Maryland to Lewes, Delaware to New York.

Nussie and I remain friends. He always finds the time to stop and shoot the breeze for a while when my friends and I show up looking for crab bait and a fishing report. To this day, I still get keyed up when I get a call from Nussie with a favorable fishing report and an invitation to go fishing. One of our most recent conversations centered on the intricacies of fishing with live bait. Nussie was telling me about the techniques he thought were necessary for success, a subject he obviously knows a great deal about. In closing, he said something that is a perfect example of his modesty. "But, ya' know, I could write a book 'bout what I don't know."

*Inside the shanty at
Scotts Cove Marina*

Fact is, Captain Robert "Nussie" Webster knows more about Tangier Sound and its ebb and flow of the tide, the comings and goings of the crabs and finfish that inhabit it, and the catching and shedding of Chesapeake Bay blue crabs than just about anybody I've ever met on or near the water.

Recently, while I was on the dock at my house in Sharptown, I checked out the two crab pots hanging from the dock. I wanted to see how many "keeper" hard crabs I had caught. While I was culling out the undersized crabs, I decided to see if I could tell if any of the crabs were peelers. There it was – a red band across the backfin of a crab. I could see the sign! It was a milestone for me. I can "read" the crabs.

# *Twentyone*

## The Bay and Beyond

My conversations with the watermen about life on Chesapeake Bay continue to take place from time to time. When asked about recent harvests and the health of the crabbing industry, Nussie replied, "It's in trouble. The annual harvest is down throughout the Bay. They can hardly make a livin' down in Saxis and things are gettin' tight in Crisfield, too. This is the only area I know of that's still doin' fair, and who knows how long that'll last."

"What do you think is causing the decline in the crab harvests?" I asked.

"Take a look around, there's a lot of stress being put on this old Bay!"

I told him about some articles I had read and some of what I had learned about this problem over the years. "Did you know," I asked him, "that industrial and municipal facilities are ALLOWED to discharge pollutants into the Bay and its tributaries, as long as they stay within Regulatory Guidelines? You would be amazed to learn what power plants are allowed to discharge into what they call mixing zones."

"Not surprised," he continued. "Add to that the fact that now everybody wants to live on the water. It all adds up. When I was little, you could scrape for crabs right here along the shoreline and in the thoroughfare and do pretty good. Not anymore."

"And I remember crabbing in the shallows near the islands with my father and brothers when the water was still crystal clear," I added.

The Bay continues to experience dead zones, algal blooms and fish kills at unprecedented levels. Large areas of the Chesapeake aren't healthy enough to support blue crabs and rockfish. Oyster harvests are at historic low levels, which put more pressure on the crab harvests to offset the loss of income to the watermen. It hits recreational fishermen hard as it gets more and more difficult to catch a few fish to bring home for dinner. It's personally upsetting when I catch a rockfish with ugly sores on it. Scientists are not yet sure of the cause of these lesions. Some suggest that overfishing the bait fish, menhaden, has greatly reduced one of the main food sources for rockfish, which results in weaker fish with lower immune systems.

There appears to be a significant reduction in fisherman out of Windsor's Marina, where recently only a couple of boats are moored – kind of lonely. The marina is silted in, making the water so shallow that many boats can't get in to the dock. Making matters worse, the less it's used, the less the little channel into the marina is kept clear. The marina is back on the market for sale.

Most scientists agree that the major problem in the Chesapeake Bay and its tributaries is pollution from nitrogen and phosphorus. They also agree on the major sources of the Bay's pollutants, which include municipal and private sewage discharges, industrial discharges, storm water runoff from roads and parking lots, agricultural runoff including golf courses and private lawns, and emissions from power plants and cars.

The amount of commercial and residential development in the Bay's watershed has resulted in a huge loss of natural buffers to filter these pollutants and a huge increase in non-permeable surface areas that channel the chemicals, fertilizers and silt into the Bay. There is also an endless list of "minor" sources of pollution in the Chesapeake Bay watershed that continue to add up. In short, the Chesapeake Bay is under assault.

I believe there is a connection between a clean, healthy environment and our physical and spiritual well being. I also believe that if we look, we could all see how our daily lives impact the Bay and its tributaries, and thus be more inclined to make changes to mitigate these negative forces, thereby maintaining or improving the Bay for future generations.

It will take a concerted effort from a majority of people to reverse these trends and to legislate change. I believe people are more likely to protect our waterways, forests and fields if they experience the natural world first hand, up close and personal. When it comes to Chesapeake Bay and its tributaries, that means getting on, in or near the water. The good news is that there are people and organizations that do care and are doing great work with positive results for the Bay.

As of April 2010, crab harvests had rebounded a bit, the probable result of tighter crabbing regulations throughout the bay area. 2011 and 2012 crab harvests were lighter. In 2013, as of this writing, crabbers that I spoke with are even more disappointed than the previous two years. The industry remains vulnerable and must be protected.

A couple years ago, planning one last fishing trip for the season, I called Nussie to check on the availability of soft crabs for bait. I knew they were getting scarce and this would be the last of them for the year. "I'll come up with somethin'," he said, and we planned to meet around one o'clock on Saturday afternoon. Jim Coffman, Bob Cannon and I were on our way and getting close to Scotts Cove when Nussie called my cell phone. "I'm headed to Wenona," he said. "I'll be back at one thirty. Do you want to meet at the shanty or why don't I just stop by your boat?"

"My boat would be great!" Sure enough, Nussie went out of his way and showed up with three dozen soft crabs. That late in the season, the bait was like gold. The weather was perfect, and we had a wonderful afternoon catching rockfish in the shallows of Tangier Sound. We would not have enjoyed such success without those beautiful soft crabs!

Thank you, Captain Nussie, for the crabs, the fishing, the friendship and the memories!

"The minute you think you've got 'em figured out,
they'll make you think you're the dumbest person on earth."

– Captain Robert "Nussie" Webster

# Chesapeake Bay Blue Crab Recipes

The blue crab. Callinectes sapidus. (Callinectes is Greek for "beautiful swimmer," sapidus is Latin for "tasty" or "savory.") The Chesapeake Bay's most valuable seafood harvest. Whether you're planning a relaxed dinner with a few friends or a big crab feast with your extended family, here are a few recipes provided by my family that we hope you enjoy.

## Fried Soft Shell Crabs

By Laurie Stephens and Nancy Stephens
Serves 3

### Ingredients

6 soft shell blue crabs, cleaned (remove lungs, face and apron)

1 1/2 cups of milk

1 egg

1 cup flour

1/2 cup cornflake crumbs

1 1/2 Tbsp. OLD BAY© Seasoning

Crisco shortening

### Directions

Whip egg and milk together (sort of like scrambled eggs). Separately, mix flour, cornflake crumbs and OLD BAY Seasoning.

Heat enough Crisco in a fry pan to cover bottom of pan with about 1/2 inch of the melted liquid. Dip crabs in egg/milk mixture, then in flour-cornflakes-OLD BAY mixture, coating both sides and all the legs.

Heat Crisco to HOT but not burning. Place crabs in Crisco and cook until crispy golden brown. Remove from pan and place crabs on a paper towel to absorb excess grease.

Eat while hot!

## Elegant Crab Soup

By Johnnie Stephens
Serves 6

### Ingredients

2 Tbsp. butter

1 1/2 Tbsp. flour

2 1/2 cups milk

1 tsp. salt

1/4 tsp. black pepper

1/4 tsp. red pepper

1 pound crab meat

1 cup cream

1 hardboiled egg

Sherry to taste (I recommend
a nice sherry, about a wine glass)

### Directions

Melt butter in sauce pan and stir in flour,
then milk, salt, and peppers.  Stir until well
heated and thickened. Add crab meat and
cream.  Heat well.  Pressing it through a
sieve, add the egg.  Add sherry and correct
seasonings, adding more salt and red
pepper if necessary.

This dish should never be underestimated.
It is simple, tasteful and delightful.

## Crabby Stuffed Mushrooms

By Victoria Stephens

### Ingredients

30 fresh mushrooms, cleaned and stems
removed

1 8-oz. package cream cheese, softened
at room temperature

8 oz. fresh crab meat, somewhat pulled
apart so it mixes well

4 Tbsp. finely minced shallots (or red
onion)

4 Tbsp. creamy horseradish sauce

2-3 dashes Worcestershire sauce

2 Tbsp. melted butter

### Directions

Blend all ingredients except mushrooms
and butter. Fill mushroom caps with
blended mixture. Drizzle melted butter
over the caps, sure to get a few drops onto
each mushroom. Bake at 350 degrees for
10-12 minutes, making sure all the cheese
is melted and the mushrooms are tender.
Serve hot.

## Crab Dip

By Nancy Stephens

### Ingredients

1 pound lump crab meat

2 8-oz. packages of cream cheese

1/2 pint sour cream

4 Tbsp. mayonnaise

Juice of 1/2 lemon

2 tsp. Worcestershire sauce

1/4 tsp. garlic salt

1 tsp. dry mustard

1 Tbsp. OLD BAY Seasoning

1/2 cup cheddar cheese, shredded

### Directions

Mix all ingredients in baking dish
including crab meat except 1/4 cup
cheddar cheese. Spread the remaining
1/4 cup cheddar cheese on top and bake
at 350 degrees for 45 to 50 minutes.
Serve with crackers or toast points.

## Uncle Bill's Sauté Crab Cakes Special

By Bill Stephens
Serves 4

### Ingredients

1 pound Maryland blue crab meat (I prefer lump back fin meat for best crab cake texture)

1 seasoning packet OLD BAY® Crab Cake Classic Mix (1.24 oz.)

1/4 cup mayo

2 bell peppers (yellow, orange or red), chopped

1/4 red onion, chopped

Fist full of chopped shallots

2 Tbsp. olive oil

1 cup white wine, preferably a good Chardonnay

OLD BAY Seasoning to taste

### Directions

Slowly sauté onion and bell peppers in olive oil and white wine. Add sprinkles of OLD BAY Seasoning.

Separately, sauté chopped shallots with a little white wine and olive oil.

Combine OLD BAY Crab Cake Classic Mix and mayo, then add crab meat as directed on the OLD BAY mix package. Add sautéed shallots to the crab cake consortium. Make 4 crab cake patties by hand. Add the crab cakes to the onion and pepper reduction in the sauté pan. Sprinkle a little more OLD BAY Seasoning onto the top of the crab cakes. Add more white wine to the pan. Allow crab cakes to simmer about 5 minutes on each side in the reduction.

Consume crab cakes. Drink a little Chardonnay alongside.

Summers in the Bay country are hot and humid. So like most summer feasts, we suggest cooking these beauties outside over a good size gas burner. Cooking inside over a very high flame will also work.

## Steamed Blue Crabs – A Celebration of Family, Friends, Food and Fun

### Ingredients

Water, enough to fill the bottom of a large pot without quite reaching up to the rack inside the pot

Cider (or white) vinegar

1 can beer

Blue crabs, enough to fill the pot

OLD BAY seafood seasoning

Pot with a raised metal rack inside, high enough to be able to boil water under the rack yet keep the crabs above the water line

### Directions

In a pot with a rack, pour in water, vinegar and beer, just enough to keep liquids below the rack. Using tongs, place blue crabs, layer upon layer, on top of the rack. Sprinkle each layer with OLD BAY Seasoning. Careful! The crabs will I be kicking. "But if they ain't kickin', you don't want to be cookin''em," as they say. Cook only live blue crabs. (Discard any others.)

Cover pot. You may want to put a brick or some other heavy object on top of the lid, in case the crabs get lively. Over high heat, bring liquid at bottom of pot to a boil. Cook until crabs turn a nice rich red color. It's about 25 minutes of cooking from the time you put high heat under them until they're done.

Remove crabs from pot with tongs, pile onto table covered with newspaper or butcher paper. Best eaten while hot.

A great Stephens family tradition, one we hope you'll enjoy, too.

## Chef Chris' Crab Cakes

By Chris Stephens
Serves 8

### Part 1 - Crab Cakes
**Ingredients**

2 lbs. crab meat

1 oz. chopped garlic

2 Tbsp. OLD BAY Seasoning

4 oz. mayo

1 Tbsp. total of chopped tarragon/thyme/sage

Pinch of salt

Pinch of pepper

**Directions**
Combine these ingredients to form crab cake patties (about 8 to 10).

### Part 2 – Cook Crab Cakes
**Ingredients**

1 cup flour

2 eggs

1 cup milk

2 cups Panco Bread Crumbs

**Directions**
Dip crab cakes in flour, THEN egg wash (egg & milk), THEN bread crumbs. Refrigerate until firm (about 20 minutes). NOTE: They'll cook much better if they are refrigerated, thus staying together better while cooking. Sauté in butter until golden brown.

### Part 3 - Chipotle Puree
**Ingredients**

3 oz. chipotle in Adobo (comes in a can)

1/4 bunch of cilantro (stemmed and rough chopped)

2 cloves garlic, rough chopped (about 1 oz.)

**Directions**

Purée in blender or small food processor until smooth.

### Part 4 - Mashed Potatoes
**Ingredients**

8 potatoes (prepared as mashed potatoes)

2 ears of corn, grilled (slightly charred is preferable)

**Directions**

Cut corn off husk. Combine corn with mashed
potatoes. Add chipotle puree "to taste" a little
at a time. Cover to keep warm.

### Part 5 - Rémoulade
**Ingredients**

1 large shallot

3 oz. cornichons or 3 Tbsp. of sweet pickle relish
or 1/2 dill pickle, chopped

1 Tbsp. capers

1/4 tsp. cayenne pepper

1/4 tsp. paprika

1 Tbsp. brandy

Pinch of salt

Pinch of pepper

1 cup mayo

**Directions**

Purée all except mayo. Put the mixture into a
mixing bowl, then fold in mayo.

### Part 6 - Chipotle Honey
**Ingredients**

1 oz. Chipotle in Adobo

4 oz. honey

**Directions**

Purée until smooth.

### Part 7 - Basil oil
**Ingredients**

1 cup loosely packed basil leaves

1 cup olive oil

2 cloves garlic, rough chopped

Pinch of salt

Pinch of pepper

Bowl of ice water

**Directions**

Blanch basil in boiling water for 10 seconds;
quick chill basil in ice water bath to keep the
color. Pat dry. Purée the basil with olive oil,
garlic, salt  and pepper.

### Part 8 - Plate Up

Spoon a portion of mashed potatoes
onto plate, place crab cake on potatoes,
then spoonful of rémoulade on top of
crab cake. Drizzle chipotle honey and
basil oil on cakes and around the plate.

*Mollies Point*

# *Bibliography*

**Books**:
Warner, William W. "Beautiful Swimmers." New York, NY: Penguin Books, 1976.

**Newspapers and Publications:**
The Associated Press. "Rockfish infected with wasting disease." The Daily Times, Salisbury, MD (12 Mar. 2006): p. A1.

The Associated Press. "Estimated blue crab harvest down; In 2007, Maryland barely tops record low." The Daily Times, Salisbury, MD (5 Feb. 2008): p. B1.

Baker, William C., "Dead Zones, Again," Save The Bay (The Magazine of the Chesapeake Bay Foundation). Summer 2007: p. 2.

Barrett, Greg. "Mercury turns fish into suspect food." The Daily Times, Salisbury, MD (16 Feb. 2004): p. 1.

Blue Crab Technical Work Group, "The Blue Crab 2003, Status of the Chesapeake Population and its Fisheries," Chesapeake Bay Commission. www.chesbay.us/Publications/Blue%20Crab%202003.pdf

Carmean Jr., Joe E. "Nitrogen discharge targeted; Salisbury wastewater plant upgrade eyed by Bay Foundation." The Daily Times, Salisbury, MD (21 Feb. 2004): p. 1.

Clines, Francis X. "Warnings Don't Sway Watermen's Faith in the Blue Crab." The New York Times, New York, NY (13 May 2001). http://www.nytimes.com/2001/05/13/us/warnings-don-t-sway-watermen-s-faith-in-the-blue-crab.html

Daly, Gay. "Hundreds of Man-Made Chemicals – In Our Air, Our Water, And Our Food – Could Be Damaging The Most Basic Building Blocks of Human Development." OnEarth (Natural Resources Defense Council). Winter 2006: pp. 21-27.

Dollar, C.D., "Reeling in Rock," Save The Bay (The Magazine of the Chesapeake Bay Foundation). Summer 2007: p. 14-16.

Duhigg, Charles. "Cleansing the Air at the Expense of Waterways." The New York Times, New York, NY (12 Oct. 2009).

The Eastern Shore News. "Company faces dredging charges." The Daily Times, Salisbury, MD (20 Nov. 2004).

Editorial. "Work together for bay crabs." The Daily Times, Salisbury, MD (25 Sept. 2007): p. A6.

Fahrenthoid, David A. "Chesapeake Bay crabs are making a big comeback." The Washington Post, Washington, DC (15 Apr. 2010): http://www.washingtonpost.com/wp-dyn/content/article/2010/04/14/AR2010041404996.html

Gates, Deborah. "Horn Point: Bay plan has little new." The Daily Times, Salisbury, MD (5 Dec. 2009): p. A1.

Montgomery, Jeff. "Laurel dumps its sewage into creek." The Daily Times, Salisbury, MD (17 Nov. 2004).

Nunley, Kate, "Bringing the Bay's Health into Focus," The Maryland Natural Resource, Maryland Department of Natural Resources. Summer 2007.

Parker, Gretchen (Associated Press Writer). "2003 Md. crab harvest may be worst in 25 years." The Daily Times, Salisbury, MD (18 Dec. 2003).

Robinson, Aleksandra (Capital News Service). "Chesapeake dead zones an economic threat." The Daily Times, Salisbury, MD (17 Sept. 2009): p. A1.

Ruth, Eric (The News Journal). "Have claws, will travel: Delmarva crabs get shipped from coast to coast." The Daily Times, Salisbury, MD (23 Sept. 2007): p. A9.

Vandiver, John. "BAY: Panel says stronger measures are needed." The Daily Times, Salisbury, MD (18 Dec. 2003): p. 1.

Williams, John Page, "WARNING SIGNS: Dead Zones, Algal Blooms, and Fish Kills," Save The Bay (The Magazine of the Chesapeake Bay Foundation). Summer 2007: p. 11-13.

**Television**:
"Menhaden: The Most Important Fish in the Bay," Prod. Center for Environmental Filmmaking, American University. Narr. Gillian Ray. Dir. Sarah Gulick. Maryland Public Television. 16 April 2012.

**Internet**:
www.dnr.state.md.us/fisheries/news/story.asp?story_id=314, "DNR Releases 2013 Chesapeake Bay Blue Crab Numbers." Maryland Department of Natural Resources (Fegley, Lynn - Deputy Director), 19 Apr. 2013.

http://yosemite.epa.gov/opa/admpress.nsf/0/8F5EF6C6955F6D2085257B52006DD32F, "EPA Proposes to Reduce Toxic Pollutants Discharged into Waterways by Power Plants." United States Environmental Protection Agency, 19 Apr. 2013.

www.epa.gov/oaqps001/gr8water/xbrochure/chesapea.html, "The Great Waters Program – Chesapeake Bay." United States Environmental Protection Agency, 22 July 2011.

www.epa.gov/cleanenergy/energy-and-you/affect/water-discharge.html, "Water Discharge." United States Environmental Protection Agency, 8 Apr. 2013.

http://www.baystat.maryland.gov/sources.html, "What is Causing the Problems." Maryland BayStat.

*Sharptown Sunset*